Be:
Live in Florida

Your guide for finding
the best place to live
in Florida today ...

Includes cities / towns ideal for
singles, couples, families & retirees

Dagny Wasil

BookSpecs Publishing

Pennsville, NJ

Best Places to Live in Florida

Your guide for finding the best place to live in Florida today

By Dagny Wasil

Published by: BookSpecs Publishing, 16 Sunset Ave., Pennsville, NJ 08070, 856-678-2186

ISBN 978-0-9903276-3-9

LCCN 2014915859

aren't limited to: loss of personal assets (tangible or intangible), information, service, profits, business, clients or other pecuniary loss. The information contained within this publication is not intended as advice - personal, consumer, financial, legal, medical, or otherwise. This publication's information is being provided for educational purposes only. The reader is encouraged to seek, the advice of a professional whenever applicable. The owner or reader of this publication assumes full and complete responsibility for any use of this material and all related information. BookSpecs Publishing does not assume any responsibility or liability with regards to these materials on behalf of the reader whatsoever.

Contents

Introduction

Where are the best places to live in Florida? If you want to know then this book has been written to help you find out.

The challenge of writing a book such as this, of course, is that what one person considers to be a great place to live isn't necessarily what another person thinks is wonderful. Some folks may prefer rural havens, while others prefer more urban settings. Still others might really only care about where they might be able to find a decent job during the week so they can plant their feet into some warm beach sand every weekend. Such criteria narrow down the list of choices for places to live.

Introduction

It's all about priorities. And when taking into consideration diverse ages and the different stages in life that readers are in, well, what then? These add another layer of complexity to the situation.

What I did was research the areas considered to be "the best of the best," meaning cities / towns that are constantly referenced — over and over again — as the finest throughout the Sunshine State. And just about all of them are ideal for residents of all ages. With that in mind, there should be enough diversity among all of the places we talk about in these pages to give you, the reader, a good idea about whether or not any place may (or may not) be a good fit for you in particular.

This book covers the 7 major geographical regions that make up Florida and then identifies those places within each region that have an ongoing track record of local fans call these areas "home." I worked hard to include, where possible, large cities, small towns and beach communities. This way, if you're attracted to a certain region you'll have a better opportunity to find a place inside it that matches your individual personal goals and lifestyle.

I hope you find my research profitable. Please consider the fact that this book isn't meant to be

Introduction

the "final word" in anyone's search for their personal "Shangri-La." It's meant to be a springboard to further reading and personal exploration that results in you actually visiting places in Florida that are most attractive after reading about them. Then (and only then) can you know for sure whether or not the reality of any actual destination mirrors its descriptions.

May this book be a useful and practical tool in your library about Florida!

Panhandle Region

The Panhandle is home to one of America's best scenic drives and breathtaking beaches. Its waters are hues of emerald and turquoise and are some of the most beautiful that Florida has to offer.

Known for its bays that breakup its white sandy beach, the Panhandle has more character in its 200 miles of coastline than almost any other part of Florida. In addition to white, sandy beaches there are lots of shore areas that feed the bays and subsequent wildlife.

Its five bays include Pensacola Bay, Choctawhatchee Bay, St. Andrea Bay, St. Joseph Bay and Apalachicola Bay. These large inlets make up the Panhandle's two distinct coasts; Emerald Coast and Forgotten Coast.

Emerald Coast covers the majority of the Panhandle's beaches and bays. It got its name in the 1980s and even though it's an unofficial name it's a perfect description of the 100 mile stretch of beautiful Florida waters. The family-friendly Emerald Coast has seen a lot of expansion and new construction in the past several years and as it continues to grow so do career opportunities, property values and residential communities.

Forgotten Coast got its name in the early 1990s when it was seen as the remaining undeveloped section of the Panhandle's coastline. It stretches from Florida's Mexico Beach all the way to St. Mark's. Tallahassee is the closest major city at about 90 miles away.

Panhandle Region

Florida's Panhandle has a rich history and distinct culture. It has a "look and feel" that is often distinctively "southern" due to its geographical proximity to southern Alabama and Georgia.

While other parts of Florida are ideal for citrus crops and stay very warm throughout the year, the Panhandle is the state's cooler region. Of course, for Florida that means the Panhandle has all of 20 cool days a year. The rest are warm and mostly sunny.

Beautiful weather isn't hard to come by here. The annual averages are highs between 77-80 degrees and lows between 53-59 degrees. This milder weather makes the northwest part of Florida ideal for those who don't want to live with Central and Southern Florida's extreme heat.

Because the Panhandle is unable to support citrus crops locals have tried other ways to grow the region's economy throughout its history. Before World War II, for example, Panhandle residents depended largely on farming, lumbering, forestry, paper mills and import/export shipping. After the war, the Panhandle's economy got a boost from newly established military bases. Tourism quickly gathered up steam afterwards, and with it, the Panhandle's hospitality industry. More recently the area has been supported by big companies like Westinghouse, Monsanto, St. Joe Paper

Panhandle Region

Company and Gulf Power who all supply a large number of jobs.

The Panhandle also has a more recent claim to fame. It's home to several military bases that have opened their doors to the filming industry. The bases have appeared in the films Twelve O'Clock High, Jaws 2 and Thirty Seconds Over Tokyo. None of this seems to have gotten in the way of the region's laid back charm though.

The cost of living in the Panhandle varies widely. While some of the places we're going to take a closer look at come in under national averages, others can be quite pricey.

Many people who move to Florida are disappointed that they can't seem to find jobs that support the cost of living in the area they've chosen to move. It's always important to research how much it's going to cost to live in a specific area before moving there.

Popular Panhandle destinations include places such as Panama City Beach, Pensacola, Tallahassee, Apalachicola, Fort Walton Beach and Destin. Some of the many area attractions include the Pensacola Naval Air Station, located right on the Gulf Coast, the nearby National Naval Aviation Museum, and Bear Creek Feline Center on Tracy Way. Locals enjoy places like such as these throughout the year.

Panhandle Region

As a resident of the Panhandle, you could plan a day trip to the Historic Pensacola Village or visit the Barrancas National Cemetery as well as Fort Barrancas, both located in Pensacola. Or you could visit the famous Indian Temple Mound Museum shows you what the Panhandle was like long before it became a destination for spring breakers and seafood lovers.

Speaking of seafood, life in the Panhandle wouldn't be complete without enjoying some of its many restaurants. Stewby's Seafood Shanty in Fort Walton Beach and Buddy's Seafood on Highway 79 are just two of the many favorites of locals. Whether you're in the mood for a seafood shack or fine dining you'll find what you're looking for in the Panhandle.

You're never short of things to do and see in Florida's Panhandle. Just off the coast of its white sandy beaches are barrier islands that make for beautiful off-shore destinations. For those who prefer a wilder side of the Gulf of Mexico, deep sea fishing is a popular activity. The beach itself is a natural playground, fun for families and adventure seekers.

As a resident it's not always the local museum or deep sea adventure that's on your to-do list. Enjoying your own town and your own backyard can make for a fun, relaxing day. There aren't too

Panhandle Region

many places in the Panhandle that are overcrowded or full of commotion either. In general, the Panhandle life is laid back and relaxed. It's ideal for singles or families who want to enjoy the outdoors and surround themselves with natural beauty and history.

Panhandle Region

Tallahassee

Tallahassee is the state capitol of Florida and is located on the northeastern side of the Panhandle, right next to Interstate 10. It is a beautiful city featuring large, swooping oak trees that cover many of the streets creating shade from the warm Florida weather.

The city is surrounded by McCain (to the west), Macon (to the north), Lafayette (to the east) and Henrietta (to the south). The city is far from the beaches of the Emerald Coast, yet has a sophisticated beauty and charm. This is especially true when viewing the state capitol building and beautifully kept parks nearby.

The city's attractions often reflect its history. An event called Living History conducts a reenactment of battles fought in the Civil War. This reenactment also includes an educational look into the lives of the Apache Indians and 17th century life. It's located at the Tallahassee Museum on Museum Drive. The museum's exhibits are an educational destination for families with children and anyone else who enjoys Floridian history and culture.

Tallahassee summers are long and hot. Like most of the Panhandle Tallahassee has a subtropical humid climate with temperatures often hovering around 100°F in peak summer. The winters are short here.   While they are cooler than many other parts of Florida you don't need much more than a sweater or light jacket to keep warm on the coldest days.

The potential for hurricanes may be of more concern to those who are considering Tallahassee as a new home. Since 1985 only one hurricane (Hurricane Kate) has struck Tallahassee directly. But others have brushed the city with their outer wind and rain bands.

Thankfully, there was generally very little damage from those storms. The most damage from hurricanes or heavy rainfall in Tallahassee often comes from flooding in low-lying areas.   This means it's a good idea to find out what areas qualify as being "low-lying" before purchasing any real estate.

Tallahassee has many job opportunities. As of July 2014 there were many publically listed jobs, including ones in accounting, health care, nursing, transportation and executive management. These were in addition to many others. Such opportunities make it a promising place to live for those who qualify and want to move to Florida.

In addition to having a variety of employment opportunities, Tallahassee also has a more affordable real estate market for those who can afford homes within the $140,000 to $250,000 range. The average listing price for July 2014 was just above $222,000. The average sales price was lower at $145,000 and had just seen a decrease of 4.7%. Tallahassee's most popular neighborhoods are Betton Hills, close to downtown and in-between Thomasville and Centerville roads, Indian Head-Leigh, located in the 32301 zip code, Piney Z on Plantation Road, Summerbrook on Preservation Road and Killearn Lakes, just north of Interstate 10.

For those who would be moving to the area with their family, the top-rated public schools are Sail High School, Pace Secondary School (3rd thru 12th) and W. T. Moore Elementary School located in the heart of Tallahassee.

Tallahassee is a city for anyone that wants to live in a thriving Florida town. At times, it's a college town, with vibrant culture, great food, and professional opportunities. At other times, it reflects the charm of a much smaller place, especially when visiting its more historical areas. But it's also somewhere that residents can access lots of great outdoor spaces.

Tallahassee doesn't offer scenic beaches or coastal attractions, although those things are certainly within driving distance. It's much more of a blend of city-rural life, which helps give Tallahassee its own distinct look and feel.

Panhandle Region

The fact this city is ideal for young professionals helps make it a wonderful home for many families. Many retirees may not be as attracted to Tallahassee as they are to some other Panhandle towns (although this writer still encourages them to check it out). Tallahassee strongly appeals to those who like the combination of modern opportunities mixed with historical architecture and old-Floridian culture. Residents here endure summer heat in exchange for the enjoyment of lovely weather and mild winters for the better part of the year.

Panhandle Region

Pensacola

Pensacola, Florida is located at the westernmost part of the Panhandle. Its waters include the Pensacola Bay and a stretch of beach along the Gulf of Mexico. It is separate from Pensacola Beach and though its beaches are beautiful they do not directly access the Gulf Coast. You can access the open sea by boat by navigating around Pensacola Beach itself, which is a peninsula separating Navarre Beach and Gulf Breeze from the ocean.

Pensacola is a hub for tourists. With annual airshows and beach activities going on all the time, Pensacola Beach is a happening, go-to destination. Non-beach activities regularly include art shows at the Pensacola Museum of Art on Jefferson Street and ballgames at the Pensacola Bayfront Stadium on W. Cedar Street. Josh Turner and other musical guests perform at Vinyl Music Hall and Pensacola Bayfront Stadium.

The average cost of living index is listed as being 88.40 as compared to the national average of 100. As of mid-2014, over 300 homes were on the market in Pensacola, with average listing prices of $211,000. The median sales price was much lower at $155,000. Pensacola's most popular zip codes are 32507 with an average listing price of $346,000, 32526 with an average listing price of over $175,000 and 32561 with the highest listing average at over $520,000.

Pensacola's two top-rated schools are Jackie Harris Preparatory Academy, just east of Interstate 110 and Sacred Heart Cathedral School, also east of Interstate 110.

As of mid-2014 Pensacola had several hundred publicly advertised job openings for qualified applicants. These included sales job opportunities, customer service job opportunities, healthcare positions and a variety of others. The top employer in the Pensacola area is Securities USA which provides monitoring, consulting and investigative security services.

As a resident of Pensacola you could start your morning on Pensacola Beach's beautiful white beach then - for the antique lovers - take a short drive to Navy Boulevard and visit Blue Moon Antique Mall and shop its 13,000 square feet of merchandise. From there you wouldn't want to miss lunch at one of the area's best seafood restaurants, Joe Patti's. (This one is an area favorite).

Once the sun goes down an active nightlife scene begins in earnest. Along the south side of Pensacola and on Pensacola Beach there are all sorts of historic venues, sophisticated martini bars and Irish pubs. Throughout the year the nightlife gets kicked up even higher with the accompaniment of various food and wine festivals.

If considering a move to Pensacola then it's important to distinguish the difference between the Pensacola mainland and Pensacola Beach. Pensacola Beach has all a good beach town offers. Those living in the Pensacola mainland drive a short distance, or take a boat ride, if they want to go to the beach.

For families able to spend over $100,000 on a home the lower average cost of living may be helpful. There are less promising job opportunities in general for young professionals who want to grow and expand on their career because Pensacola is very much a smaller town in that regard. But many retirees love Pensacola. It offers nearby beaches, wonderful shopping and a slower than average pace of life.

Panama City

Panama City has been called the "Playground of the Gulf Coast". It's located along US Route 98, along the Gulf Coast, just about right in the middle of the Panhandle region. This makes its white sandy beaches part of Emerald Coast. The entire city is just over 29 square miles with a population of around 35,000.

The people who call Panama City home enjoy a warm, subtropical climate that can be a bit humid, but is generally much milder than Central and Southern Florida. The winters are mild and short while the summers are hot and sunny.

Obviously, a Florida winter in this town doesn't compare to a northern winter. A light jacket is all you would need to keep warm on the coldest of Panama City days. As for the summers, keeping cool is a breeze with the beach always nearby.

Thankfully the 2010 BP oil spill didn't have a drastic impact on Panama's beautiful beaches. The most damage it did was a few small oil spots just off the coast that were quickly cleaned up and disposed of.

The phenomenon known as the red tide, however, does keep residents vigilante of their local waters during the summer months. The red tide is an algae bloom that sometimes happens in these waters. Even though Panama City hasn't been drastically affected by it residents generally keep out of gulf waters when warned. This bloom can cause respiratory problems in some people even when it's mostly offshore.

There are career opportunities in the area for those who have the education and skills to match them. Gulf Power and Rock-Tenn are two local companies that help supply jobs to many area residents. The Bay Line Railroad and Panama City-Bay County International Airport bring in tourists year-round also, which attracts money to stimulate the local economy.

As for the events, Panama City doesn't disappoint. The year starts off with a bang at the 800-pound Beach Ball Drop on New Year's Eve along the boardwalk at Pier Park. The Pirates of the High Seas Festival is an annual event as well and this beach town wouldn't be complete without an annual Lobster Festival and Tournament. But beach activities aren't the only way to enjoy Panama City. There are plenty of activities to keep everyone in the family busy.

When the streets aren't filled with tourists awaiting the unleashing of 10,000 bouncing balls on New Year's Eve at the annual ball drop they're typically quiet and laid back. Middle Beach, East End and Pier Park all have the tropical themed retail therapy a shopper's heart could desire. When you're done shopping you could do what other locals do and enjoy the piers, water activities and nightlife.

When it's house-hunting time there are a variety of markets to pick from. Panama City's housing market currently has nearly 1,000 homes for sale with an average listing price of just over $236,000. The most popular neighborhoods are Bunkers Cove, King Estates, Venetian Villa, Magnolia Terrace and Bayside. It was a buyer's market in 2014 for those shopping within the $200,000-$250,000 price range. Even though the market had seen listing price increases of 1%-2% it also saw a drop in sales prices of over 6% as of June of 2014. This made for better buying opportunities for those who could afford the lower prices.

There are many elementary, middle and high schools in the area for families with children. They are a part of the Bay District Schools and collectively have over 30,000 students. The highest rated school in the area is North Bay Haven Career Academy. The next best rated schools are Jinks Middle School, Bay High School, Rutherford High School, Everitt Middle School and Merriam Cherry Street Elementary.

Panhandle Region

Panama City is advertised to be a "family friendly" place with lots of things to do. In addition to beaches, there are nearby parks, and practically endless spots to go hiking, biking, canoeing, kayaking and more traditional variations of boating,

Whether you're single, newly married, have a sprouting family or are ready to retire, Panama City generally can offer its residents either lots of activity or a more laid back lifestyle with a sometimes lively flair. It's definitely one place to check out if these possibilities appeal to you.

Panhandle Region

Fort Walton Beach

Fort Walton Beach is just east of Pensacola and sits right on the shores of Choctawhatchee Bay. It is sandwiched between Walton County (east) and Santa Rosa County (west). It is a thin stretch of land that runs along the Emerald Coast, has crystal like waters and white sandy beaches.

Fort Walton is a beach resort community with year-round fishing. Summer is its busiest time of the year when thousands of people come to the Emerald Coast to enjoy the subtropical weather. Spring break is also a busy time for Fort Walton Beach. Spring Breakers enjoy staying at the beachside resorts and lining the beach during the day.

Like much of Florida, Ft. Walton Beach has very hot and humid summers. Its summers last from May to September and have highs in the high 80s and 90s. Autumns and winters are also generally warm and the coldest winters get are in the 50s and sometimes high 40s.

As of July 2014 Fort Walton Beach's average listing price is approximately $258,000. The median sales price for Fort Walton Beach was up 2.6% (as of July 2014) - approximately $155,000. The most popular zip codes were 32578, 32548, 32547, 32536 and 32539. The listing price averages for these zip codes was between

$166,000 and $400,000. Zip codes 32539 and 32536 had the lowest averages starting at $166,000.

Schools in the area include Fort Walton Beach high school which is a public high school that caters to grade 9th through 12th, St. Mary School which is a Catholic school catering to PK-8th grades and Okaloosa Academy which caters to 6th through 12th grades. For parents moving to the area they will be pleased to find all of these schools located in Fort Walton Beach.

Nursing and other medical positions are available in Fort Walton Beach for those who qualify as well as a wide variety of other career opportunities. While job opportunities can be somewhat varied Fort Walton Beach is dedicated to economic development and has put in place many business incentive programs to encourage growth in the area. This development started in 2010 and continues today. As for its current economic state, Fort Walton Beach's unemployment is just below 5% as of early 2014.

With its beach resort community status the area brings in many tourists and for those who qualify for hospitality jobs there are opportunities that arise throughout the year. Some residents also work outside of Fort Walton Beach in surrounding areas such as West Pensacola and Freeport.

Panhandle Region

For young families Fort Walton Beach offers nearby schools and a leisurely outdoor lifestyle. For the business professional the area offers a place to call home that is in close proximity to other cities, which offers them a wider source of job opportunities.

Retirees should be aware that Fort Walton Beach is a mix of activity and tourism. There are lots of things to do, especially for those who love an outdoor lifestyle. But one must also accept that this town is regularly filled with the hustle and bustle of tourists and spring breakers.

There are waves of people who make this place their temporary destination every year. But many full-time residents love this area for its aqua-blue waters and vacation-influenced atmosphere. Golf courses, parks, aquariums and museums are all a part of this famous tourist town that is also happens to be a great place to live in Florida.

Panhandle Region

Destin

Destin, Florida is just slightly east of Fort Walton Beach. It is a stretch of Peninsula sandwiched between Fort Walton Beach and Miramar Beach. Destin is surrounded by the waters of Florida's Emerald Coast and the Choctawhatchee Bay. When you approach Destin traveling eastbound on Highway 98 it looks like an island completely surrounded by gorgeous blue water.

Destin is especially popular because of its 100-Fathom Curve. The 100-Fathom Curve is what draws deep-sea fishers from around the country. In fact, Destin has over 4.5 million visitors each year.

Why do people choose Destin to experience the 100-Fathom Curve, which comes closer to Destin than any other spot of land on the Gulf Coast? A fathom is a measurement of 6 feet making the fathom curve 600 feet deep and teeming with varieties of fish and other marine life. There is no other experience like it in any other part of Florida.

Fishing isn't the only activity that residents enjoy, however. Divers can plunge up to 90 feet to explore artificial reefs, a limestone shelf and shipwrecks. If you're lucky you'll also spot a pod of dolphins in the bay. They will often play in between the crab boats and snorkelers.

Panhandle Region

The average cost of living is 120.60 compared to a national average of 100. This means that Destin is quite an expensive place to live. Real estate in Destin is especially on the pricey side when compared to most other cities in the Panhandle.

The average listing as of July 2014 was quite steep, at over $650,000. Buyers who are unable to spend a half a million dollars or even a quarter of a million for that matter will have to do in depth research to find a property or rental in their price range. The median sales price however is much lower at $227,000. This average appeals to more buyers who are looking to spend much less than the average listing price.

Popular zip codes in Destin are 32578, 32548, 32547, 32536 and 32539. These zip codes areas feature homes with average listing prices between $166,000 and $338,000 with 32539 … and 32536 having the least expensive averages, which are between $166,000 and $195,000.

If you're looking to move to Destin and have a family then you should know there are just three schools located in the town (as of 2014). Destin Elementary School, Destin Middle School and Destin Christian Academy are the three choices parents have. Destin is also zoned, however, for Freeport High School (K-12) which located in Freeport about 45 min outside of Destin.

Panhandle Region

This city is definitely a place kids can enjoy though. All summer long there are arrays of local summer camps. Summer WILD Children's Summer Camp is a five day long camp at HarborWalk Village for 1st-6th graders. The local drama camp located at Destin Elementary School has a theme each year, with 2014's being "The Wizard of Oz". A kid's summer art camp is held each year at the Arts and Design Society Center in Fort Walton Beach and those are just a few of the kid-friendly activities that the area offers.

Because of its 4.5 million yearly visitors, job opportunities in Destin - for those who qualify - are largely hospitality based. There are 52 hotels in the area as well as fishing, boating and water sports companies. Since the beginning of 2014 the unemployment rate has dropped from 5.0% to 4.4%. As the economy recovers and the 2010 oil spill scare subsides, vacationers are coming back and more job opportunities are becoming available too.

For most, Destin is a vacation destination rather than a hometown. But this means residents are seldom short on things to do, especially during the summer. Summertime is especially fun for local children who enjoy the summer camps and beach with the rest of the family.

Panhandle Region

Overall, Destin is a lively and exciting town with beautiful beaches and outdoor adventures. If Destin is your choice for your next move then be ready for a slightly more expensive housing market in order to pursue a high lifestyle that includes lots of sunshine.

Panhandle Region

Apalachicola

Apalachicola is approximately 80 miles southwest of Tallahassee and located in Franklin County, Florida next to US 98. It sits right at the Apalachicola River and is only 2.7 square miles with approximately 2,300 residents. Apalachicola is generally humid and subtropical with average highs in the 80s and average lows in the 50s.

People who live in Apalachicola generally prefer the quieter part of the coastal life. Commercial fishing boats for shrimp and oysters leave their docs in the mornings to begin another day out at sea before returning later in the day. The downtown traffic is sparse and directed by one traffic light. And just north of the town are Goat Island and Saint Marks Island; both of which keep Apalachicola relatively secluded from East Bay boat traffic.

Town residents do enjoy putting on events. The Full Moon Climb takes place at the Cape St. George lighthouse where the general public and members of the St. George Lighthouse Association enjoy the view of the full moon from the top of the lighthouse. There is also an annual Chamber of Commerce Golf Tournament for business members from Franklin, Gulf, Leon and Wakulla counties. For those who enjoy scary adventures, the Chestnut Creek Cemetery offers ghost walks and tales of what life in the area was like more than 100 years ago.

The average cost of living is listed as being 98 (as compared to the national average score of 100), which means it's a slightly less expensive place to live. This rating discounts the cost of real estate though.

Apalachicola's real estate market went through a drastic change at the beginning of 2014. The median sales price for a home jumped an astounding 253.0% and in July of 2014 was at $350,000. The average listing price went up as well to about $262,000.

Apalachicola isn't necessarily the area for a businessman or businesswoman looking to expand will want to relocate. A big city environment would probably be better. It's definitely a small town with a small-town lifestyle.

The income per capita is about $16,000 as of May 2014 and the unemployment rate was 5.6%. While it is a beautiful town many working locals have jobs outside of Apalachicola in the surrounding Franklin, Gulf, Leon and Wakulla counties in order to make a living.

Parents who are interested in moving to the area have several schools to choose from. Apalachicola Bay Charter School, First Baptist Christian School,

Panhandle Region

Franklin Company Public School, Bay Community School and Chapman Elementary School are all located within Apalachicola.

Apalachicola isn't the place for great beaches or for being a spring break destination. It's a beautiful, simple, relatively quiet small Florida town surrounded by wildlife and calm waters. It offers a laid back lifestyle with very little commotion year in and year out.

The look and feel of this place is probably more like Cape Cod than Deep South. But if you like friendly old fishing towns then you're going to love Apalachicola. Remnants of old Florida's fishing, oyster and timber industry are all around, as are the nearby inlets and shallow bays one would expect to find.

With many acres of national and state forests to explore, close beaches just a short drive away and some of the finest seafood around, it's not hard to see why many people are naturally attracted to Apalachicola. Those who stay, however, especially like the quiet charm and friendly atmosphere found here.

Northeast Region

Imagine a part of Florida where you can enjoy sun-soaked beaches, the nation's oldest city and beautiful horse-filled countryside all in one day.

Northeast Region

For northeastern Floridians this place exists. This part of Florida has a variety of venues like no other part of the sunshine state. It's simply full of beautiful sites and cultural places.

Northeast Florida's cities include Jacksonville, Ocala and historic St. Augustine, among others. Its coast was discovered almost 450 years ago when Ponce de Leon came in search of The Fountain of Youth. Needless to say, he didn't find it, but he did discover what is now known as Florida. The northeastern coast is nicknamed "The First Coast" and is home to the oldest European settlement in America.

When people talk about the northeast part of Florida they're referring to the counties of Flagler, St. Johns, Bradford, Putnam, Clay, Alachua, Clay, Duval, Nassau, Baker and Columbia. The northern border of the northeast of Florida runs next to the Georgia line and the east side of the northeastern area is the coast of the Atlantic Ocean.

Though it is a part of Florida and experiences Florida's subtropical weather, with long hot summers and short warm winters, much of northeastern Florida doesn't look very tropical. There are plenty of palm trees, but they are heavily mixed in with mature oak trees and tall pines that make up the foliage.

Northeast Region

Not only is the area rich in flora it also appeals to many career-minded individuals in the state. The city of Jacksonville offers many job opportunities to apply for. Those who meet qualifications can find sales jobs, management positions and opportunities in many areas of health care. The top employers in the Jacksonville area are Armellini Express Lines, CHI Payment Systems and Firestone Complete Auto.

The news isn't as promising for many of the local public school districts in the area, however. As of July 2014 the northeast school districts were experiencing mixed results from elementary and middle school testing. More schools than ever received an "F" grade. Among the best performers were charter schools. But many private school options are available for parents nowadays, including home schooling. Many thousands of families home school throughout Florida, including the northeast region.

Duval County is home to Jacksonville, the biggest Florida city, and many people choose to move here for its many perks, including job opportunities and housing. Other area perks include two outstanding colleges nearby.

The University of Florida (home of the Florida Gators) is located in Gainesville. It is Florida's largest and oldest university and the pride of the northeast. Jacksonville University is the area's leading school of nursing, with degrees in becoming an RN, BSN or MSN.

The first quarter of the NE Florida real estate overview of 2013 showed an average home sales price of just above $188,000. This was a 10% increase from the year before. The highest numbers of sales were of homes between $40,000 and $50,000. The most number of homes for sale were in the $200,000-$250,000 price range.

Since the economic downturn of 2008 the market has continued to recover with higher asking prices and more homes slowly being listed. This isn't necessarily the best news for new home buyers coming to the area, but the inventory does give buyers a variety of prices and home types from which to choose.

Much of the northeastern part of Florida is considered the "greater Jacksonville area". The Port of Jacksonville in located on the St. Johns River and helps support most of this area. Over 100 countries use the Port of Jacksonville to import and export goods. It imports the 2nd largest number of vehicles on the east coast. And a 63,000 square foot area is reserved for cruise ships, which have been operating in the port since

2003. Cruises often leave from Jacksonville to visit the Bahamas and other places.

Living in the northwestern part of Florida gives locals a variety of destinations to enjoy. If you want to visit America's oldest city it's a leisurely drive south to St. Augustine. For those who prefer the downtown of a big city, Jacksonville has award winning restaurants like Blue Bamboo on Southside Blvd and an exciting nightlife.

Jacksonville Beach and Amelia Island, which is just northeast of Jacksonville, offer very popular beaches. And the Ocala countryside, where Triple Crown winner Affirmed was bred, is well-known to horse lovers all over the country.

No other part of Florida seems to offer such a wide variety of landscape, employment, entertainment and outdoor activities. Northeastern Florida has a lot to offer residents. Many people that move here each year end up making it their permanent home.

St. Augustine

St. Augustine is located just south of Jacksonville, Florida (about a 45-minute drive away) and just north of Daytona Beach (also about a 45 minute drive away). It's a beautiful old city that claims many of America's "firsts."

The first house ever built in the US still stands in the heart of old St. Augustine. A short walk through the town will lead you to the first schoolhouse ever built in America also. From there you can visit the St. Augustine Fort that was built right next to the shore so any threats from foreign ships coming into the harbor could be seen miles away.

St. Augustine is home to Flagler College, which also gives it somewhat of a college town feel. So many tourists visit St. Augustine on a regular basis, however, that much of the foot traffic in town is a mixture of tourists, college students and other area residents.

To this day St. Augustine still offers carriage rides that take visitors through the inner part of town, including the local winery and other establishments among its historic streets. While St. Augustine does have its own beautiful beach, the shoreline of downtown St. Augustine is muddy and rocky.

The average cost of living index for St. Augustine is rated at 103.20, compared to a national average of 100. This means that it is slightly more expensive to live in St. Augustine than the average American town.

St. Augustine does have some affordable reasonable real estate though. Many homes can be found in the $100,000-$200,000 price range, although there seems to be far fewer homes on the market than can be found in many other cities. This could pose a problem for anyone looking to move to the area. Many people could find it harder to obtain suitable housing with smaller numbers to choose from.

There are three public schools in St. Augustine that include one for every age range. St. Augustine High School caters to 6th through 12th grade. Wards Creek Elementary School offer classes Pre-K thru 5th grade. And Sebastian Middle School fills out the list for children schooling the years in between.

St. Augustine offers fewer job opportunities than most places, especially for career-minded residents. This leads many St. Augustine locals to find work in nearby Jacksonville. Most of these workers are able to commute to their jobs in about an hour or less. As a result many people in the northeast view St. Augustine as a weekend getaway rather than as a great place to live in itself.

Those who can afford to live here and support themselves economically are able to enjoy the many local events that play on the city's rich history. There are even Spanish ships docked in the harbor downtown, with regular historic weapons demonstrations also available at Castillo De San Marcos.

Every 2nd Saturday of the month downtown St. Augustine features city walks and pet friendly tours. It is also home to an IMAX theater showing recent movie releases and documentaries. Those who like spooky adventures you can tour the city's lighthouse at night, take a ghost tour ride through town or tour the old cemetery.

Departing from downtown, one notices that homes and businesses are spread relatively thin around the rest of St. Augustine's area. It's simply a beautiful place for those who want to live among the sights and culture of old America, including those who desire a smaller town atmosphere.

While St. Augustine may not be a good place for everyone, especially those who aren't economically prepared or independent, it's hard to beat for its beauty, history and cultural amenities. Many retirees will certainly want to visit here before deciding to live somewhere else in Florida.

Northeast Region

Palm Coast

The city of Palm Coast, located in Flagler County, is just south of St. Augustine about 20 minutes north of Daytona Beach. It is one of the newest of Florida's cities, just having been incorporated back in 1999. Palm Coast is billed as an ideal place to enjoy outdoor spaces and also get in touch with nature. Many tourists visit here each year in order to go golfing and also take one of the many eco-tours that can be found throughout the area.

The area around the city has 70 miles of freshwater and saltwater canals and intercostal waterways. For those who enjoy trails, Palm Coast has over 125 miles of connecting paths for walking and bicycling. These trails are lined with beautiful, old oak trees and large pine trees that offer outdoor enthusiasts lots of shade from the hot Florida sun.

Fishing and boating are enjoyed year-round thanks to Palm Coast's long summers and relatively short winters. Bird watching is also a popular activity around Palm Coast's parks and beaches. The trails here were designed specifically to lead walkers and bikers through some of the most beautiful parts of the area. There are lots of opportunities to spot seabirds and dolphins playing in the waters along with the intercostal waterway.

Northeast Region

The area's cost of living index, based on the US average of 100, is 96.30. This means that it is less expensive to live in Palm Coast than the average US city. The average real estate sales price in Palm Coast was just over $140,000 as of July 2014. The average listing price in Palm Coast during July was $332,000.

If you're considering Palm Coast as your next home you should be able to find real estate that fits your needs searching within some of the most popular zip codes. Zip code 32137 has average listings of about $425,000, while the zip code area of 32110 had homes for sale in the $120,000 range. There were thousands of homes on the market at this time as well.

It may be a bit difficult for most workers to find work in Palm Coast, as the number of job opportunities are much fewer and far between than a big city like Jacksonville. In July 2014 publically listed career employment included openings for skilled labor, health care, customer service, sales and management. Companies in the area who frequently hire include Sunbelt Chemicals Corp. and Consulate Health Care.

For those who have children in school, Flagler County Public Schools include 18 schools that offer public education throughout the area. The top-rated public schools in Palm Coast are

Phoenix Academy High School and Lewis E. Wadsworth Elementary School.

Palm Coast offers residents an ideal location to live in between the historic city of St. Augustine and the event-filled city of Daytona Beach. Although unskilled, skilled and professionals may find it a bit difficult to find a job that suits their needs within the city itself. Many residents are still attracted to Palm Coast because it offers more affordable home prices than many other places nearby. Lower real estate prices, along with lower than average living costs, are especially beneficial to many singles and young families.

It may not be an overstatement to say the most appealing aspect of Palm coast is its location. What other lovely cities are sandwiched between the most historic city in America (St. Augustine) and the birthplace of racing (Daytona Beach)?

While Palm Coast is generally regarded as having a slower pace than many other Florida cities, it offers locals many outdoor adventures, including a wonderful beach life. Many Palm Coast retirees enjoy living in a quieter place that has access to a larger number of sights, activities and amenities within short driving distances.

Ocala

Ocala Florida is located right in the middle of Northern Florida just south of Gainesville. Ocala looks very different from the rest of Florida. Instead of the flat land Florida is known for, Ocala has rolling hills and beautiful countryside.

It actually looks similar to areas within the state of Kentucky in this regard. There are beautiful horse farms throughout Ocala and many of the country's top racehorses are bred and born here, in the heart of the Marion County. Among the most well-known horses is the Triple Crown winner Affirmed.

Ocala's tourist destinations include nearby Silver Springs, also located in Marion County, where visitors enjoy cool, clear waters and mossy landscape. Water recreation includes swimming and glass bottom boat tours. The Ocala National Forest between the Ocklawaha and St. John's rivers and the Wild Waters waterpark in Silver Springs are also popular local destinations.

The average July high is 91.7°F and generally hot and humid. Ocala's location towards the center of the state is one reason why its temperatures are among the highest in the state during the summertime.

Ocala basically has two seasons. The first is the dry season, which takes place from October to May. During this season there is very little rain and just about every single day is bright and sunny. The second season is the wet season, which happens between June and September. The warmer weather helps spark thunderstorms that occur almost daily.

Storms in Ocala can be severe. This area is known for having more lightning per square mile than almost any other city in the world. Wet season temperatures typically range from lows in the 70s to highs in the 90s.

The area's cost of living index is relatively low at 85.90. This is in comparison to the national average of 100. Ocala had average real estate listing prices of $325,000 as of the first week of July 2014. Between April and July 2014 the median sales price in Ocala had an increase of 13.4% and was at $149,000. The most affordable zip code in the area is 34472, with an average listing price of $93,000.

The Ocala area has fewer job opportunities than most other places in northeast Florida. But there are always open positions in sales, healthcare, customer service, management, information technology, retail, engineering, skilled labor, banking, automotive and manufacturing, for those who qualify.

The school district for Ocala is Marion County Public Schools. Marion Technical Institute is a top-rated high school that teaches 11th through 12th grades. South Ocala Elementary School, located on SE 24th Rd., has PK-5th grade students and Ambleside School of Ocala, located on Se Broadway Street just south of Highway 40, has K-8th grade students.

The Appleton Museum of Arts located on Silver Springs Boulevard puts on many downtown areas events each year including educational art films, historical exhibits, art exhibits and receptions. In addition to art-based events Ocala is known for its many horse-related events, including annual horse shows.

If you love the countryside and are looking for a beautiful area to call home then Ocala may be the place for you. It offers affordable homes, a generally lower cost of living, and job opportunities for professionals and others with in-demand skills. Many individuals, families and retirees enjoy living here.

Jacksonville

Jacksonville is the largest city in Florida by population and has the largest city area in the United States. Downtown Jacksonville sits along the St. Johns River. Its north and south banks have a laid-back atmosphere with urban vibe.

During the work week professionals enjoy dining destinations for unique lunches and fill the streets throughout each day. The thoroughfares are also filled with visitors enjoying world-class museums, casual bars, upscale lounges and a variety of dining options.

Jacksonville has 22 miles of lovely beaches that offer visitors and locals a variety of water activities include fishing, kayaking, paddle boarding and surfing. You can also travel a short drive north to the historic area of Mayport, which has seafood restaurants and casino boats. Just south of that are the communities of Neptune Beach and Atlantic Beach, each featuring shopping and upscale dining restaurants.

At the heart of Jacksonville Beach visitors fill sunny days with water activities and picnicking on the sand. The Jacksonville Beach Fishing Pier is usually lined with fishers pulling in catches and people enjoying the ocean views from above.

The average cost of living index is 90.60 compared to the national average of 100. This means that it is less expensive to live in Jacksonville than the average US city. Jacksonville has very affordable home prices for those shopping within the $100,000-$200,000 range. The average listing price in Jacksonville, as of mid-2014, was $224,000 and the median sales price was much lower at $136,000.

The area's most popular neighborhood was Mandarin with an average listing price of over $500,000. Riverside is the next popular neighborhood with average listings at around $400,000. Chimney Lakes is also an attractive neighborhood for many buyers with average prices starting just over $160,000.

Because of Jacksonville's size and continuous growth it has many opportunities for professionals. As of July 2014 the area featured hundreds of publicly advertised jobs related to sales, healthcare, customer service, retail, skilled labor, finance and engineering. In total, Jacksonville itself had over 1,900 job listings.

For those moving to the area with children Jacksonville has several schools with good ratings, most of which are located east of Interstate 295. The public high schools in the area are River City Science Academy right at the corner of Highway

90 and Beach Boulevard, Duval Virtual Instruction Academy located on Prudential Drive and Bishop John J. Snyder High School west of Interstate 295. Pace Center for Girls-Jax (right in the heart of Jacksonville) and St. Paul Catholic School on Park Street are two of the area's finest elementary and middle schools.

Some fun facts about Jacksonville are that it is home to the oldest skating park in the US -- Kona Skatepark located in Arlington. Before he was famous, skateboarder Tony Hawk competed there.

Jacksonville's other claims to fame are several movies that have been filmed in the area including Why Do Fools Fall in Love, The Creature from the Black Lagoon, GI Jane and The Adventures of Pippi Longstocking. Some rock & roll fans may even remember Elvis Presley performing in his first indoor concert at Jacksonville's historic Florida Theater in the late 1950s.

With relatively uncrowded beaches, access to the Atlantic Ocean, and an established cosmopolitan nightlife, Jacksonville is a popular place to both live and visit. The city is also home to the largest urban park system in the country; there are 10 national and state parks touching it.

Northeast Region

Jacksonville is a city for those who crave a busy, active lifestyle. It's a great place for budding professionals, families and those who want the benefits of a big city with nice beaches nearby. There is nothing "laid-back" about this place. There is something always happening here for residents of every age.

Gainesville

Gainesville is a college town at heart. It is home to Florida's largest and oldest university and is the nation's eighth largest campus based on enrollment. The city is especially known for the importance its residents place in preserving its historic buildings and its natural surroundings.

Thousands of visitors and locals enjoy its many parks, lakes and museums. Gainesville residents claim it's one of the most attractive cities in Florida because of its urban forest and beautiful landscape. National Geographic Adventure even ranked Gainesville as one of the top cities in the United States to live and play.

The average cost of living in Gainesville is indexed at a rating of 89.90 compared to the US average of 100. This means that it is less expensive to live in Gainesville than the average US city. Homes in Gainesville averaged $218,000 (listing average) in 2014 and sold for a median sales price of $133,000 as of July 2014.

For those shopping for homes under $100,000, some of Gainesville's most popular neighborhoods had affordable prices. Highland Court Manner had average listing prices of just over $60,000, the neighborhood of Duval had average listing prices under $60,000 and Turkey

Northeast Region

Creek Forest on NW 13th Street had average prices of just over $80,000.

In keeping with Gainesville's tradition of quality learning, its surrounding public elementary, middle and high schools also have good reputations. Expressions Learning Arts Academy caters to K-5th grade and Oak Hall School, located west of Interstate 75, hosts Pre-K thru 12th grade. The area's Catholic school is St. Francis Catholic High, also located west of Interstate 75 and not far from Oak Hall School.

Shands Hospital at UF and the University of Florida itself are the leading Gainesville employers and provide jobs for many of the residents, including many in surrounding counties. For those qualified in medical, teaching and administrative careers, Gainesville is one of the best places in Florida to find work.

The biggest events in Gainesville happen when the Florida Gators play a home game. College football fans across the whole town rally around their college team and cheer them on. Gainesville also has a number of big name music artists who often come to town as a stop in their tours. Country favorite Jake Owen is just one of the many artists who will perform at the Stephen C. O'Connell Center.

Northeast Region

While Gainesville isn't near any bodies of water, it does have beautiful landscape. Big, shady trees are sought out by individuals in order to help them cool off during the hot summer days. Temperatures often reach highs in the 90s but many residents can still be found enjoying the outdoors.

Many people flock to Gainesville to experience the benefits of a college town. But they also come to the area to enjoy its historic downtown and to experience many of the area's yearly events.

Its downtown is lively and features businesses, eateries, museums and galleries. There is a rich cultural, artistic and historical environment here. But there is also lovely natural side to the city. Kanapaha Botanical Gardens, for example, contains 62 acres of specialty gardens and forest areas.

Gainesville may not be an ideal city for retirees who prefer a quieter life. Big football games, for example, typically result in cheering fans and traffic jams. On the other hand, some retirees actually enjoy the liveliness and amenities found here. And the lower cost of living is welcomed by every resident, including singles and those making up young families.

Northeast Region

Gainesville is an especially ideal city for young adults because of its University life. But its world-renowned hospital is a draw to many others too. As a major employment center, many great career opportunities are available in Gainesville. Top professionals are a part of the fabric of its community.

Amelia Island

Amelia Island is, as its name suggests, an island. It's one of the southernmost islands among the See Islands - a cluster of barrier islands that stretch along the East Coast of Florida all the way up to South Carolina - and is 13 miles long and about 4 miles wide at the widest point.

Amelia doesn't have quite the look you might imagine when thinking about how a typical island might appear. It features lots of large old oak trees hanging over narrow roads, with moss drooping from their branches. There is a decidedly casual, laid-back southern feel about this place.

Fernandina Beach and Amelia City communities are both located on Amelia Island. In addition to the island's 13 miles of beautiful beaches it also has abundant wildlife surrounding its warm waters. The area is loved so much by locals and visitors it was voted as one of the Top 10 North American Islands by the Conde Nast Traveler's Reader's Choice Awards for seven consecutive years.

The average listing price for Amelia Island homes in July 2014 was over $900,000 and the median sales price was $500,000. Amelia Island is prime real estate with beautiful homes along its coasts. If these prices are not within your budget there are nearby zip codes that have much more affordable asking prices. Zip code 32046 had the lowest prices in the area with an average listing price being just over $137,000. The next higher priced zones were located within zip code 32011, with average listings at $165,000. All of these zip codes are located near Fernandina Beach.

The area cost of living in 2014 was listed at 118.50 as compared to the US average of 100, meaning it's much more expensive to live there than in the average American city. Job opportunities for Amelia Island residents also include those within Jacksonville because the city is so close (about 30 miles).

This close proximity to the larger city of Jacksonville gives residents the ability to live in a more laid-back town while working in places that can be reached just a short driving distance away. As of July 2014 Amelia Island area job opportunities included sales jobs, management positions, customer service jobs and healthcare careers, among others.

Local schools for Amelia Island residents include Southside Elementary School on Jasmine Street and Fernandina Beach High School located on the east side of town. While real estate shopping you could also look for homes zoned for any of the other 21 schools within the Nassau County School District.

Many Amelia Island residents start each year with an annual New Year's Day Feast at Jack & Diane's Cafe in historic downtown Fernandina. And later in January Amelia Island restaurants participate in the Annual "Amelia Island Restaurant Week," where diners tour some of the islands finest eateries. During the same week Amelia Island plays host to the Zooma 5K and Florida Half Marathon. The local Jack & Diane's Café sponsor the Valentine's Love Fest in downtown Fernandina, with lots of food and wine available for diners. In addition to these fun events there are events such as book festivals, film festivals and music festivals held throughout the year.

Amelia Island is a beautiful place to live with many events to keep its residents busy. Most locals enjoy living in a place that offers the look and feel of a laid-back island while also having access to the amenities of a big city such as Jacksonville. If financial resources aren't a hindrance then it's truly one of the nicest places in Florida that just about any single, couple, family or retiree could possibly live.

Central West Region

Central West Florida can also be referred to as The Tampa Bay Area. Its definition varies depending on who you ask, but most everyone can agree that the greater Tampa Bay Area consists of St. Petersburg, Tampa, Clearwater, Sarasota and their surrounding metropolitan areas. The area also includes Old Tampa Bay, Middle Tampa Bay, Lower Tampa Bay and Hillsboro Bay.

Tampa Bay is a large harbor along the Gulf of Mexico comprised of the above listed bays. Until the early 20th century the Tampa Bay waters were full of fish and wildlife. The people of Safety Water - the Native Americans who lived in the area - lived off huge schools of mullet, shellfish, manatees, sea turtles and crabs. Even during the late 19th century people still witnessed schools of mullet swimming in the bay that were so large many boats had to navigate around them.

Before the Safety Harbor culture lived in the area, approximately 2,800 years ago, the Weeden Island culture inhabited the Tampa Bay area. Their sites were found in Tampa Bay and Mobile Bay where they lived, hunted and fished.

Not much is known about those cultures. When Spanish explorers arrived in the early 1500s they found villages around the northern part of Tampa Bay and another cluster of villages along the southern part of the bay. The area had a rough start with settlers who almost completely abandoned the area when the Second Seminole War started.

During the American Civil War the area was no more than an outpost. Martial Law was declared in 1862 and the city's government ceased operations for the rest of the war. By the time the Reconstruction period rolled around Tampa still had very little industry. It struggled during this time and stayed nothing more than a fishing village, with just a few people living there. It wasn't until the late 1800s that things began to turn around. Phosphate was discovered in the area and, soon after, railroads made their way to the town.

In the early 20th century the US Army Corps of Engineers started dredging operations in Tampa Bay to make it navigable for commercial shipping. Today, thanks to these deeper water channels, Tampa Bay is a port for seaborne commerce. The Port of Tampa is now the largest in Florida and the 10th largest port in the nation.

The Tampa area has nearly 4.2 million residents nowadays. Its sports teams include the Tampa Bay Buccaneers (NFL), the Tampa Bay Rays (MLB) and the Tampa Bay Lightning (NHL). Sports, however, are not the reason most people come to Tampa.

Tampa itself sits tucked away within the bays. St. Petersburg and Clearwater make up the furthest cities west whose coastlines meet up with the Gulf of Mexico. From Tampa you can travel North on Interstate 275 to reach Clearwater and St. Petersburg. From there you can travel by boat out to the many islands including Treasure Island and St. Pete Island. To travel further south you need to get back onto Interstate 275 and cross the mouth of Tampa Bay.

The greater Tampa area has the long hot summers and short winters that Florida is known for. While it can be rather enjoyable to live somewhere where you don't have to shovel snow, Tampa weather can be very humid and muggy in the summer. Average summer highs reach the high 90s, with nighttime summer lows dropping down to the mid-to high 70s. From November to February daytime temperatures drop to the high 70s and you might need a light sweater in the evenings because of temperatures dropping to the 50s.

The greater Tampa Bay area has some of the most beautiful beaches in all of Florida. USA Today named Clearwater Beach the "Best Beach Town" in 2013. Locals enjoy its family-friendly beaches and the pier where you can fish off the sides.

Fort DeSoto Park was named one of the top 25 beaches in the US and "Best Family Beach" by USA Today. As beautiful as these beaches are there is nothing more serene than Caladesi Island State Park located just west of the mainland. This three-mile beach can only be reached by boat and is one of Florida's last undeveloped barrier islands. Spending a day on its deserted shores can wash all of your worries away. Beautiful towns and beach havens literally run all the way down the Gulf side of Central West Florida. Most locals who love the beach seem to have their favorite spot.

Central West Region

About an hour south of Tampa is the beautiful city of Sarasota. It too features its own award-winning beach areas, especially Siesta Key. But Sarasota features great amenities, including lots of commerce, culture and food. It's as easy to find an upscale restaurant in Sarasota in order to get something to eat as it is to find a local dive or pub. And locals seem to have their pick of some of the best supermarkets and specialty food stores found anywhere.

There are beautiful places to see and something to do practically everywhere you go in Central West Florida. This is one reason why many retirees seem to be drawn to this area. This particular area also seems to be very attractive to "snowbirds" from up north who visit from November through April.

The area of Tampa is one of the few places in Florida you can enjoy a big city, diverse commercial operations and beautiful clear waters available within relatively short driving distances. Having these amenities, among many others in one area, is what makes Tampa and its surrounding areas appealing to so many people.

Central West Region

Tampa

Tampa is located on the west coast of Florida, on the Tampa Bay and near St. Petersburg. The city sits on the Gulf of Mexico but is blocked from direct access to the open ocean by its famous bay.

Tampa has a number of sports teams which make for a variety of year-round sporting events. Their current teams are the NFL team Tampa Bay Buccaneers, the Tampa Bay Lightning NHL team and the Tampa Bay Rays, which are the local major league baseball team.

The downtown area of Tampa is generally considered to be the beautiful part of city. It has a distinct skyline of tall buildings and is easily accessed by Interstate 275 and Interstate 4. There are also a couple scenic bridges crossing over Old Tampa Bay giving access to the main traffic arteries into Tampa from places such as St. Petersburg and Clearwater.

Ybor City is known as Tampa's Latin Quarter. It is a historic neighborhood located northeast of downtown. La Setima is the main street for most of the activity in that section of the city. Live music pours out of the patio bars and nightclubs into streets that are lined with art galleries and eclectic shops and eateries. A variety of restaurants in Ybor include Cuban, Italian, Spanish, French and Greek cuisine.

The city has won its share of awards. In 2008 Forbes magazine named Tampa as the 5th best outdoor city. The Washington Square News newspaper named Tampa a top city for young professionals. And the Pew Research Center did a study that resulted in Tampa being named the fifth most popular city that people want to live in after visiting it.

Tampa's average price of living index was 90.40 percent based on a US average of 100, as of mid-2014. This means that the cost of living is lower here, on average, than most other places in the US.

Tampa's real estate market often features thousands of homes at any given time. Its average listing price increased 10% between April and July 2014, raising it to over $318,000. At the same time the median sales price had a decrease of 1.1% to $160,000. Its pricier real estate market would pose a problem for anyone with a lower budget. Tampa does, however, seem to have a popular neighborhood to cover just about every price range.

One of the more affordable ranges of homes (among its most popular neighborhoods) can be found in Old Seminal Heights, located right next to Interstate 275, with an average listing of $164,000. Another popular neighborhood is Tampa Palms, located between Interstate 275 and Interstate 75, having an average listing price of over $370,000. One of the most expensive neighborhoods is Davis Islands. It has an average listing price is over $1.1 million.

For those with children considering moving to the area, La Voy Exceptional Center is one of the area's top-rated schools, located in West Tampa. Its two top-rated private schools are Holy Trinity Lutheran located in the southwestern part of Tampa and Anointed Word Academy, located closer into town on the east side of Highway 92.

Tampa media typically features lots of advertised job opportunities for people with a variety of career qualifications. These jobs especially included those in healthcare, sales, business support skills and customer service. The largest employer in the area is Humana. UnitedHealth Group, Kelly Services and Verizon Wireless are also large employers in the area.

Tampa is a vibrant, big city that offers many amenities and events for the whole family. Some famous Gulf beaches are a relatively short driving distance away, especially Clearwater. But on hot summer days, anyone could also enjoy the indoors of the Florida Aquarium, located in downtown Tampa.

There is a lot of wonderful food in Tampa too. Many locals enjoy 5-star meals at the famous Columbia Restaurant on 7th Avenue. But local ethnic eateries abound throughout the entire area.

After the sun goes down, whether you're single, newly married or need a night out on the town without the kids, there are always plenty of nightlife opportunities throughout Tampa. The Blue Martini is just one of the many stops locals make when in search of some evening fun.

Tampa's large size often appeals to singles, young couples and families alike. It's a great place for anyone that wants access to all of the good things Florida has to offer within the setting of a big city.

Seniors who enjoy the arts, annual events and the hustle and bustle of the big city are often attracted to Tampa after searching for an ideal place to retire. The area is filled with popular retirement communities.

The main appeal of Tampa for most residents who love it, however, is that it's a large city with a rich culture and lots of things to do. When coupled with warm Florida weather and lovely beaches nearby, it's perfectly understandable why many residents consider Tampa a great place to live.

Central West Region

Clearwater Beach

Clearwater Beach has just what its name describes – beautiful, clear, blue-green tinted waters. Its subtropical weather, short winters and long, hot summers make it a year-round destination for tourists and exciting place for residents to call home.

Just off the coast of Clearwater Beach's white sandy shore pods of dolphins regularly swim and play in the waves. If you want to get up close and personal with the dolphins there are several day cruises that will take you out to see them. Calypso Queen Cruise can be boarded at the Clearwater Beach Marina, as can a boat from Classic Cruises. Not only is the area home to these wild creatures, it's also home to a famous dolphin named "Winter," the star of the popular movie Dolphin Tale. This dolphin star can be visited at the Clearwater Marine Aquarium.

Because dolphins are so near and dear to Clearwater's heart, a lot of artwork featuring them have been created and designed by local artists. Over fifty 6-foot-tall fiberglass dolphin statues stand at the Clearwater Marine Aquarium. One day, they are destined to be returned to their sponsors for display around the city to make it even easier for the public to admire.

Central West Region

Special events are a common occurrence in the Clearwater area. It's possible to check the Internet in order to see what is going on in Clearwater at any given time.

Many events often geared for tourists are also popular among local residents. You could, for example, watch beautiful sunsets at Pier 60 just about any evening. A nightly celebration begins at the pier about two hours before sunset and lasts up to two hours afterwards. Live entertainment, featured artisans and street performers are regularly featured here.

Another event that happens each week is the Clearwater Farmer's Market, which can be found downtown at the 600th block on Cleveland Street. In addition to farm fresh produce and fresh flowers, this farmers market showcases lots of specialty foods, including unique cheeses and wide varieties of fresh baked goods.

One popular monthly event is something called "Blast Friday." Clearwater participates in this one along with the towns of Osceola and Ft. Harrison. Blast Friday is basically a festival that promotes various local wines, foods and merchandise ... all for sale of course.

Clearwater's real estate market includes homes in the 33763, 33764, 33755, 33761 and 33756 zip codes. The least expensive of these ZIP Codes is

33763 with an average listing price of $98,000. The ZIP Code with the highest average listing price is 33756 at $452,000.

The average listing price for all of Clearwater Beach, as of 2014, was just under $250,000. This included an increase of over 20% at the beginning of 2014. But the median sales price dropped 23% during the same period to about $100,000.

The average cost of living in Clearwater is rated 93.40 out of a US average of 100. This means Clearwater is a somewhat less expensive place to live than the average US city.

If you're willing to make the drive, living in Clearwater also means you have the opportunity to apply for jobs within the Tampa and St. Petersburg markets. Within these job markets there are always sales opportunities, healthcare positions, customer service jobs and management positions, among many others.

Life in Clearwater Beach life is generally regarded as a mix of fun and laid-back ... depending upon one's preference. Many retirees love this area, in addition to families looking for someplace with a smaller beach town vibe that is actually very close to larger cities.

Apart from year-round tourists, Clearwater streets aren't exceptionally crowded and everyone on the beach has room to stretch their legs. A day in the life of a local might include a morning walk on the beach, lunch at a small restaurant downtown and an afternoon or evening at Pier 60, watching either the sunset or dolphins playing in adjacent waters.

Clearwater is a charming locale offering lots of outdoor fun and things to do. In addition to the wonderful beach, both residents and tourists alike enjoy the many events held in town each year. It's a pleasurable, albeit less crowded, place to live. With close proximity to large cities such as Tampa, it's also somewhere that singles, families and retirees all seem to like.

Central West Region

Bradenton

Bradenton is located directly south of Manatee River. It is both a mainland and a Peninsula connected by Cortez Rd. that bridges the two together. One thing that makes Bradenton unique is that it's part city, part suburb and part beach town. Its west side is lined with sugar-white sandy beaches and beautiful turquoise water, especially on Anna Maria Island and Holmes Beach.

In the northwest part of the city is downtown Bradenton. It is home to office and government buildings including the tallest – Bradenton Financial Center. Its eastern side is becoming a more heavily populated part of town. The most popular subdivision on the east side is Lakewood Ranch with seven villages and several varieties of home styles.

Bradenton's average cost of living is 96.30 out of a US average of 100. This means that Bradenton is a slightly less expensive city to live in vs the average US city. Its average real estate listing, as of 2014, was slightly over $300,000 and its median sales price was $150,000. The area's least expensive zip code was 34205 with an average listing price of $130,000.

Retirees can save on home buying expenses by considering one of the many retirement communities in the area, including: Holiday

Retirement, Summerfield Retirement and Westminster Communities.

For those who are considering moving to the area with children, Manatee Virtual Instruction Program is a top-rated school in the area. This school is a bit different from most and can be done by children at home. The area isn't home to a top-rated public high school. It is, however, home to a variety of elementary schools and private schools located within Manatee County.

Bradenton's career opportunities also include jobs in St. Petersburg because of its close proximity. A forty-five minute drive on Interstate 275 will get you from one to the other. As of July 2014 Bradenton and the St. Petersburg area had hundreds of publicly listed job openings in the healthcare, sales, customer service, management, insurance, nursing, retail, skilled labor and information technology categories.

The area itself doesn't feature much nightlife or tourist attractions. But it is within driving distance to St. Petersburg and the greater Tampa area, which have those sorts of things in abundance.

Apart from the sand and surf, local residents enjoy events such as seeing local artist Scott Curts sing at the Anna Maria Oyster Bar. Or they might visit exhibits at places like the Art Center Manatee, located on 9th Street. These are the sorts of things Bradenton offers both residents and guests on any given weekend. But there is plenty to do throughout the wider area within relatively short driving distances.

Bradenton's charms lie in its location. It offers access to beaches that are notable for their natural beauty, including local wildlife, but it's also relatively close to major cities, job markets and commercial centers. It's also generally a less expensive place to live along the Gulf Coast. These are the sorts of things that make Bradenton an attractive place to settle for many people.

Residents do enjoy the old Florida history, small museums and downtown Bradenton, which features a popular RiverWalk and Village of the Arts. But they really like the fact that this city is a well-placed hub for the entire central-west region of the State. This makes Bradenton a wonderful point to access places to work, plus a wider variety of Floridian cultural attractions and outdoor activities.

rsburg

St. Petersburg is just south of Clearwater and is almost completely surrounded by water. On its east side is Old Tampa Bay, which connects to Tampa Bay and flows out into the Gulf of Mexico.

Coming from the east you can enter St. Petersburg via Interstate 275, which runs directly through the city and back out at its southernmost part crossing back over Tampa Bay. On its west coast St. Petersburg is a scatter of peninsulas and islands that run along down its entire west coast.

The Central Business District is located in downtown St. Petersburg and has high-rises for business-commerce offices. There are also an array of galleries, cultural venues and prominent museums in the same area. These include both the Florida International Museum on 2nd Avenue and the St. Petersburg Museum of History also located on 2nd Avenue. Such institutions are the main reason why St. Petersburg is considered to be a major cultural center on Florida's west coast.

For those who can afford real estate in the $100,000 in $200,000 range, St. Petersburg had a selection of hundreds of homes available as of July 2014. The average listing price in St. Petersburg was just under $140,000. Its median sales price saw an increase between April and July 2014, bringing it up to $107,000. The area's most popular zip codes were 33710, with an average listing price of $252,000, and 33705 with an average listing price over $190,000, and 33713 with the lowest listing price average at $136,000.

For families with children the top rated schools in the St. Petersburg area are Mount Vernon Elementary School near the south end of St. Petersburg on 13th Ave. North, the School of the Immaculata, also located on the same street and Brighton Preparatory School, on Central Avenue.

The average cost of living in St. Petersburg is 89.40 compared to the US average of 100. This means that St. Petersburg is a less expensive place to live than the average US city.

The city has many career opportunities because of its close proximity to Tampa. As of mid-2014, St. Petersburg residents who qualify could apply for thousands of sales positions, healthcare positions, customer service positions and management positions. The top employers in the area are Humana, Verizon Wireless and Consulate Health Care.

St. Petersburg has quite an eclectic mix of attractions and events. Sunken Gardens is 4 acres filled with over 50,000 tropical plants, a butterfly garden and walk-through aviary. The Interstate 275 Bridge, which is 4.1 miles long and one of the largest and longest suspension bridges in the

Western Hemisphere, is one of the major gateways to some of the Florida's other major attractions, often available within a short driving distance.

Baseball Boulevard is lined with home-plate plaques that each have a part of St. Petersburg history and its resident's love of baseball written on them. Tropicana Field has the Tampa Bay Walk of Fame that recognizes dozens of sports legends who have called the greater Tampa Bay area home.

St. Petersburg has humid, subtropical weather that results in a rainy season from June to September. It does occasionally see the effects of tropical storms and hurricanes but the last time a hurricane directly struck the city was back in 1921. Average highs for the area are 80s and 90s during the summer and 70s to 60s in the winter.

St. Petersburg is a great place to live because of its own amenities in addition to its close proximity to Tampa and other area attractions. There are many local job opportunities and generally affordable real estate market for those in the middle class.

If you're focusing on expanding upon a career then you have the opportunity to work within St. Petersburg itself or the larger city of Tampa, just a short drive away. For families St. Petersburg offers top-rated schools and lots of fun in the area, including quick access to wonderful beaches.

Whether moving to St. Petersburg for a career or retirement or to raise a family, the city has more than enough to keep everyone busy. It's a beautiful place for those who want to enjoy a fast-paced local life, intermingled with tourism and access to other great places along Florida's west coast.

Sarasota

Sarasota sits within Sarasota Bay. Just to the west of it are some of the prettiest barrier islands in all of Florida, including Lido Key, Otter Key and Bird Key.

To reach the beach locals simply hop on one of the main thoroughfares that easily take them to any number of places along the shore. It's not hard finding a pretty beach anywhere near this city. They literally run all up and down the shore along Sarasota's west side.

As for Sarasota itself, there is an older part of the city and a modern newer part along the waterway. Its streets are often a mix of businesses, condos and local places to eat. The view of Sarasota Bay and nearby Keys, whether on the ground or atop one of the new skyscrapers, would be ideal for a postcard.

Sarasota's real estate prices, as of mid-2014, ranged from the mid-90s into the millions. The area's average listing price was just over $625,000. Its median sales price was much lower at $212,000. Both its median sales price and average listing price saw an increase in the beginning of 2014.

Bayou Oaks was the most economically priced among the most popular neighborhoods in

Sarasota, with an average listing price close to $94,000. Lido Key was a much more expensive area to live in, with an average listing price of $1.5 million. The Indian Beach neighborhood came in just below that with an average listing price of $1.4 million.

Sarasota has two public school districts. Within Sarasota, schools are either zoned in the Manatee County Public School district or the Sarasota County Public School district. The highest-rated of the local schools are the Sarasota School of Arts and Sciences, located west of Interstate 75, Brickhouse Academy for grades 6th-12th also located west of Interstate 75, and The Achievement Center of Sarasota on Lincoln Drive, west of Interstate 75.

Sarasota's overall cost of living is 96.20 based on a US average of 100. This means the Sarasota is generally less expensive than the average city. As of July 2014 Sarasota's job opportunities included sales positions, healthcare positions, customer service opportunities, management opportunities, over nursing jobs, among many others. The top employers were CHI Payment Systems, ResCare and Macy's.

Sarasota does offer its share of career opportunities. Although some young professionals may find more in a bigger city like

Tampa, there are lots of professional careers and service-related jobs in the Sarasota area. And for those who would need to shop for a home in the $100,000 range Sarasota's real estate market can still deliver.

Outdoor activities are popular in and around the entire Sarasota area, especially boating. The Intercoastal waterway and nearby keys offer some of the most attractive places to go both kayaking and power boating. It's possible to kayak in the midst of thriving wildlife and million dollar homes on the same outing.

There are lots of wonderful places to eat in Sarasota. Whether a person is attracted to unique, local venues, restaurant chains or exclusive 5-star experiences, Sarasota features them all in abundance. And if you'd like a taste of fine bistro-type fare at a reasonable price, then be sure to visit Morton's Gourmet Market on Osprey Ave. It's a favorite for area residents!

For the retiree this city offers beautiful beaches and many attractions to enjoy with the grandkids. Those who love Sarasota do so for its lower than average living expenses with the perks of having lots of beautiful beaches nearby. Not all Florida cities offer such reasonable housing prices so close to 5-star beaches.

Central West Region

A day in the life of a local in Sarasota might include a morning stroll on the sand along a shore, an afternoon visiting the turtles at the Mote Marina Laboratory and then dinner at someplace like Barnacle Bill's Seafood restaurant. For those who enjoy a little nightlife, an evening drink at The Gator Club might be a good way to end the day.

Central West Region

Valrico

Valrico is in close proximity to Tampa, about 30 minutes away and on the east side of Interstate 75. Like its neighbor to the west, Bradenton, Valrico is a rather small city with a mix of businesses and neighborhoods sprinkled throughout its small area. It has a low population density, which is a big plus for many residents who want to live in a congested area or tourist spot.

There are several features that draw new residents to Valrico. One is the fact that it offers those living here a modern suburban lifestyle without the congestion of a large city – although Tampa and St. Petersburg are relatively short drives away and Orlando just a bit further. Another thing residents frequently mention is the weather. Although summers are hot and humid, the fall, winter and spring seasons are nearly perfect in Valrico. Days are filled with bright blue skies, low humidity, pleasant breezes and occasionally chilly temperatures (especially at night).

Residents also enjoy living in small neighborhoods and close knit communities here. The public school system is considered one of the best in the state. And a wide variety of family-oriented events take place during the year in all types of private, religious and athletic organizations throughout the area.

For families considering moving to the area, Bloomingdale High School gets very high academic ratings from public schooling parents. The school has also won state championship titles in boys' soccer, girls' soccer, cheerleading and softball. With their strong reputation in sports it makes sense that notable alumni include ESPN sportscaster Erin Andrews, LPGA professional golfer Beth Bauer and NFL football player Chad Bratzke.

Valrico itself tends to offer fewer job opportunities, but lots of places to work are available in larger surrounding cities, including Tampa and St. Petersburg. For those willing to make a little bit of a drive each day they have the opportunity to find a career in one of those major commercial centers. For those who qualify, as of July 2014, publicly advertised jobs in the area included: sales opportunities, healthcare positions and customer service opportunities, among many others. The top employer for the area is Humana, who regularly advertises openings for skilled employees.

The overall cost of living in Valrico has a score of 102.30, with the US average being 100. This means it costs slightly more to live in Valrico than the average US city. As of mid-2014, the area's average real estate listing price was just over $263,000 and the median sales price of a home was nearly $230,000.

Valrico is simply considered by most of its residents to be a nice, quiet area with big city amenities close at hand. There is ample shopping and entertainment all within short driving distances and much larger cities are just a little further. There is a reason why the population here, though still small compared to many other places in Florida, has grown over 40% since the year 2000. If the idea of an upscale Florida suburb with great weather appeals to you then you'll want to check out Valrico.

Central West Region

Venice

Just south of Sarasota lies Venice Florida. Venice is a quiet and low-key town with picturesque white beaches and palm trees lining the streets. Downtown buildings are also true to the subtropical vibe that is so characteristic of this area, with painted whites, yellows, corals and greens visible just about everywhere.

At the heart of downtown is Venice's beloved gazebo where events are held on the local lawn. Only a few stop signs keep the traffic at a leisurely pace through the downtown streets. Cars are often parked parallel along these thoroughfares while residents and tourists shop for tropical themed gifts and eat at local restaurants.

Sharkey's is a favorite seafood restaurant located on the 700-foot long Venice Fishing Pier. It is the only restaurant in the Venice area that is on the beach. The pier is so popular that it even has its own website with a photo gallery and calendar of events. Large saltwater fish have been caught off this pier, including an occasional shark. What makes this pier so popular with locals and visitors is that there are no fishing licenses required. People can fish all day long and restock on bait at Papa's Bait Shop nearby.

After a day of fishing you can play volleyball on one of the two sand courts or have a picnic at one of the six picnic shelters while you watch the sun set right next to the pier. Manatee, dolphins and seabirds are common sightings playing in the clear Gulf Coast water.

Venice's real estate prices have averaged between $150,000 and $300,000 in recent years. The average listing price in Venice in July 2014 was just over $268,000. The median sales price rose to $170,000.

As of mid-2014 the listing prices were a bit steep for buyers who didn't want to spend over $150,000. The number of homes on the market, however, gave buyers a healthy inventory to look through. The least expensive of its most popular zip codes was 34232, with an average listing price slightly over $197,000.

For those with children who are considering moving to the area, there are high-rated schools to choose from. Top public schools include Venice Elementary and Venice Senior High.

The average cost of living in Venice is 99.80 out of the US average of 100. This means that Venice is slightly less expensive than the average US city. As of mid-2014, job opportunities in Venice included sales openings, healthcare positions, customer service jobs, management opportunities, nursing positions, retail jobs openings and a variety of others. The biggest employers in the area are Suncoast Roofing Supply, Macy's and Verizon Wireless. For those who qualify for these types of positions and are moving to the area, job opportunities are promising; there seem to be quite a few to choose from. Because of Venice's close proximity to Sarasota some of the listed job opportunities were in the Sarasota area.

Venice typically plays host to lots of local activities and events. Every weekend Venice puts on its weekly Farmers Market, located downtown at the 200th block of West Tampa Avenue. Occasionally free Friday night live concerts are also held downtown at the Centennial Park Gazebo. A wellness fair is held every August at the Venice Community Center. And those who love antique car shows can attend the American Antique Auto Car Show at Centennial Park. Om addition, Venice also hosts a variety of art festivals, seasonal festivals and food and wine festivals.

With over 14 miles of beaches, Venice offers plenty of recreational fun, including swimming, fishing and boating. Beach exploring and shelling are also a favorite pastimes. Fossilized shark teeth can be found in abundance in area sands.

There are a few upscale pastimes too. Venice is obviously named after the famous Italian city with the same name and there is lots of Italian-style architecture in the area. There are also more than a few scenic backdrops for golfers in the area, who typically feel right at home on Venice courses.

Venice Florida would be great for anyone who wants to live in a relatively quiet and low-key town right on the beach. Singles, families and retirees all love this place. Real estate costs a little more throughout the area, but the trade-off is getting to live in a charming town with a famous pier, weekly events and lots of southern hospitality. Venice is the sort of place where residents can go swimming in warm Gulf waters and then come and sit in the grass while listening to live music being played in the downtown gazebo.

Central East Region

Central East Florida is also referred to as Greater Orlando, Metro Orlando or the Orlando metropolitan area and includes the following counties; Lake, Orange, Osceola and Seminole. Its largest cities include Orlando, Sanford and Kissimmee, and its famous cities are Orlando (The Theme Park Capitol of the World), Daytona Beach (The Birthplace of Racing) and Cape Canaveral where the space shuttles are launched.

Much of Central East Florida is wetlands. A major drainage project in the 1880s helped make the land suitable for settlement. The terrain is flat and low and has hundreds of lakes, rivers, creeks and springs.

Central East Region

The bedrock in the Central-East region of Florida is mostly limestone which is very porous and Orlando has experienced several newsworthy sinkholes in recent years. The most widely remembered sinkhole occurred in the town of Winter Park and was simply referred to as "The Winter Park Sinkhole".

Orlando was once named Jernigan, after Aaron Jernigan, who was a cattleman. He had acquired the area of Orlando by homesteading the land as a "first settler" and used the property in his cattle business.

The name Orlando came later in honor of Orlando Reeves who ran a plantation and sugar mill near what is now Lake Eola. This lake is a still a local body of water that many residents still enjoy to this day.

During the Industrial Revolution, Orlando was Florida's largest inland city and became a popular destination between the years of the Spanish-American and World War War I. The Florida Land Boom at the time was good to the Orlando area and helped further support its quick development. When hurricanes hit the area in the 1920s, and the, Great Depression started, the boom came to an abrupt halt.

The city eventually began recovering in the following decades and in 1965 it got an announcement that would change the entire area. Walt Disney announced that he planned to build Walt Disney World in Orlando. Just three years earlier Orlando international Airport had been built and the combination of this airport with the new entertainment park would spark a boom for the Central-East area's economy that has been going on now for decades.

While Orlando was growing Daytona Beach was also experiencing growth of its own. In the late 1800s businessman Henry Flagler brought the railroad to Daytona. But the area sparked unique interests.

Visitors to Daytona Beach began attempting to break land speed records. In the early 1900s, for example, William Vanderbilt drove his race car down Daytona's wide, smooth beach, with its compact sand, and set an unofficial speed record of 92.307 mph. Racing has been associated with the city since those early days of car racing.

In recent years, a $400 million project has been launched to add to Daytona's appeal as an internationally famous tourist town. The International Speedway - brought to life by the beach racers of the area's early years - will be able to seat an additional 100,000 fans in the not-too-distant future.

Central East Region

Cape Canaveral is another unique area in Central-East Florida. During the 1500s the Spanish explorer Pedro Menendez was shipwrecked wrecked off its coast and established early ties with the Ais Indians, the native tribal group at the time. This eventually paved the way to an agreement with the tribe to be paid for the return of other sailors who had become shipwrecked in the area.

In the early 20th century, a group of wealthy journalists started a community at the Cape called "Journalista Beach". They built houses in the area and started a publication that would eventually pave the way for what is now known as the Orlando Sentinel newspaper. Their investment in the area, however, helped create a push among investors for the Cape's development as a port. The US military later chose the area as a base for military operations around 1950. The Cape's famous missile launchings at Kennedy Space Station later followed.

Big events bring guests to Central Florida. At the time of this writing Orlando is the second most popular travel destination in the country; it's second only to Las Vegas. Daytona Beach and the surrounding areas also attract millions of travelers each year.

Central East Region

Orlando's theme parks provide family entertainment and vacation experiences for entire families, while NASCAR races keep targeted fans coming to Daytona Beach, often repeatedly. But these cottage industries have created a broader influx of people, industry and markets to the entire area, which is obviously more than theme parks, fast cars and missile launchings. Many Florida residents live and in the Central-East region.

Tourism obviously makes up a large portion of Central Florida's economy. Yet Orlando continues to display a growing industrial and research base too. Educational programs, including ones from the University of Central Florida, are also experiencing growth.

Orlando has also become a center of the financial industry. A large group of local insurers and banking companies have moved to the area and provide jobs for thousands of area residents. There are also high-tech research and development companies that now make this part of Florida their home.

Let's now specifically take a look at some of the best cities and towns to live in the Central-East region. Each of them reflects both the heritage and ongoing development of this unique section of Florida.

Orlando

Orlando is a major city within Central Florida. The Greater Orlando area has a population of over 2 million people and is the 26th largest metropolitan area in the US. The area attracts over 51 million tourists every year and is known as "The Theme Park Capitol of the World".

Orlando has a humid and subtropical climate with two major seasons. It's hot and rainy season lasts from May until September and has highs in the high 90s. Its dry season is still very warm with temperatures no lower than the 70s and 80s, but the less frequent rainfall helps lower the humidity levels making the area feels a bit cooler.

The majority of Orlando is wetlands that are made up of many lakes and swamps. The land is low and wet, spotted with hundreds of little lakes. There are over 115 neighborhoods in all of Orlando. It also has 19 skyscrapers; most of which are located downtown. Even though its lands are generally wet, Orlando has built a beautiful city and quite a name for itself.

For families with children, it would be hard to convince them that there is any other place as fun and magical as Orlando. On any given day locals can visit Walt Disney World, Universal Studios, Islands of Adventure or Wet N' Wild Water Park.

Central East Region

All of these attractions are clustered together about 20 miles away from downtown Orlando.

At the heart of Orlando is Lake Eola. This small lake is a staple of Orlando with its beautiful fountain and skyline of business buildings in the background. The entire city has an upscale urban feel. If you love to shop you would never run out of stores to visit. The Mall at Millennia is an upscale mall on Conroy Road and only one of the many malls in the area. What you can't find at The Mall at Millennia you will be sure to find at The Florida Mall on Orange Blossom Trail.

Orlando also has a charming and historic side. Winter Park Florida is just slightly north of Orlando. Its downtown is lined with upscale boutiques, elegant shops and gift stores shaded by its thick, tall and mossy trees. Orlando locals enjoy Winter Park for its laid-back atmosphere and beautifully kept downtown.

For young professionals and career driven businessmen and women Orlando is home to almost every industry someone could qualify for. The hospitality industry is a big part of the Orlando culture as is the technology industry which employees over 53,000 people.

As of mid-2014 Orlando had 2,500 job opportunities including sales positions, management opportunities, customer service, healthcare positions and information technology opportunities.

The average cost of living in Orlando is 91.50 compared to the US average of 100. This means that it is somewhat less expensive to live in Orlando than the average US city. The average listing price in Orlando is $275,000. The median sales price is $165,000. If you're looking for homes under the $100,000 price range you can look in one of Atlanta's most popular neighborhoods, Pine Hills. In Pine Hills the average listing price is $80,000.

This city is ideal for professionals who want the opportunity to apply for a promising career. It is also a fun place for families to live because of its theme parks. Retirees who prefer a big city over a small beach town will enjoy the local shopping and nearby Winter Park. Orlando is unique because of its large size and many attractions.

Central East Region

Winter Haven

Winter Haven is in the middle of Central Florida with Tampa to its west and Melbourne to its east. Many of its easily accessible lakes, ponds and rivers are both popular and beautiful. These waters are often home to beautiful Cyprus trees, which help foster ideal habitats for alligators. Gators are frequently seen sunning on the banks and swimming in the many bodies of waters in and around Winter Haven.

Despite the presence of alligators, one of the more popular sports in the town is waterskiing. Waterskiing shows were once the main event at Cypress Gardens, a well-known theme park that contained a beautify botanical garden near Winter Haven. Cypress Gardens operated from 1936 to 2009. Its gardens are still around, but are now part of the new Legoland Park. Legoland features a "Lego toy" theme for its rides, catering to families with children ages 2 thru 12.

Winter Haven has a variety of events for every age group including young adults and retirees. Every Thursday the Winter Haven Farmers Market sets up at the Downtown Trailhead Park. On weekends, you could enjoy occasional live music at Central Park or a Crossfit competition at Chain of Lakes Stadium.

Central East Region

Parents in Winter Haven are often pleased to find that kids have their own variety of events that go on year-round. For example, LEGO Club starts at 4 PM every Tuesday at the town library and is a fun event that invites youngsters to use their imagination. Fizz, Boom, Read is an annual summer library event that encourages children to get excited about reading. And when families want to cool off from the hot Florida weather they can visit Legoland's water park.

There are also tons of sports activities for residents of every age – both recreational and competitive. Baseball, basketball and waterskiing, however, are probably the town's most notable recreational sports.

Winter Haven is especially appealing to anyone that wants to live on budget or just save some money when it comes to the cost of living. The overall average cost to live in the area is rated 84.70 compared to the national average of 100. This means that Winter Haven is fairly less expensive place to call home than the average US city.

The local real estate is affordable for those who want to spend less than $100,000. The average listing price is a bit higher at $178,000, but the median sales price comes well below $100,000 at $89,000. One of the most popular and affordable zip codes in the area is 34758, which has an average listing price of $137,000.

Winter Haven is an ideal "central" location in the State of Florida. It's relatively short driving distance to either Tampa or Orlando give residents access to both the job opportunities and amenities found in those cities.

The entire area in and around Winter Haven teems with water and wildlife. Its 50 lakes are a natural habitat for fish, gators, blue herons and bald eagles alike. These lakes are also world-renowned for being one of the best places to go bass fishing on the North American continent.

Winter Haven is a diverse community comprised of families and individuals. It offers residents a great place to live, work and play in the heart of Florida. Opportunities to work, recreate or simply enjoy nature while being the member of a large town are part of the everyday experiences that most people who live here really like.

Central East Region

Daytona Beach

Home of the "World's Most Famous Beach", Daytona Beach is part mainland and part peninsula. It has humid subtropical weather with summer temperatures reaching the high 90s. Summers are long and winters are very short. Cool days with temperatures below the 80s are few and far between in this part of Florida.

Why is its beach so famous? Its hard-packed sand can hold the weight of motorized vehicles. The beaches that are now lined with parked cars were once areas where car races were held for over 50 years. After a 50-year stretch of beach racing the Daytona international Speedway was finally built. Today, over 200,000 NASCAR fans come to Daytona in order to watch the racing season's opener - the Daytona 500. This race and many others are held at the Speedway year-round. Many locals, as well as vacationing visitors, enjoy this incredible spectator experience.

When Daytona Beach isn't packed with NASCAR fans it's also hosting annual motorcycle events. Over 500,000 bikers ride into Daytona for "Bike Week" in March, "Bicktoberfest" in October and the "Rolex 24 Hours of Daytona" event. The Rolex is a 24 hour long race of endurance held every January.

Central East Region

For those who enjoy shopping, the Volusia Mall is located on International Speedway Boulevard. And many antique stores and small boutiques are located on Beach Street. Beach Street is the old part of Daytona Beach where cars can still park on the side of the road and the buildings feature a popular art-deco vibe. From Beach Street one can head east on I92 for a mile before reaching the beach.

The cost-of-living average in Daytona Beach is 85.00 compared to the national average of 100. This means that it's generally less expensive to live in Daytona Beach than the average US city.

The area's real estate market had an average listing price of $126,000 in mid-2014. The median sales price stood at $67,000. The most popular zip code was 32174, with an average listing price of $256,000. The most expensive zip code in the area was 32169, with an average listing price of $475,000.

While the listing price averages are rather high for those who do not want to spend over $100,000, the median sales price is much lower and proves that there is real estate in the area available under the $100,000 mark.

Daytona was hit hard by the economic downturn of 2008. The beachside still had many closed-down shops and tourist attractions at the time of this writing. This setback, however, didn't slow all of Daytona down. The Speedway has been undergoing a massive addition of over 100,000 seats. And in addition to those new seats, the Speedway also launched a three-year, $400 million renovation that will include a large hotel overlooking the Speedway, complete with its own stores and restaurants.

Daytona's appeal is in its year-round events, drivable beaches and well-developed downtown that includes an indoor shopping mall, several well-developed strip malls and an array of restaurants.

For retirees the quieter side of Daytona is the beachside and areas along the peninsula. Those who live here are usually able to navigate around the bumper-to-bumper traffic that comes to town at certain times throughout the year. Many residential property owners in Daytona found that it was still possible to be close to this unique beach and still find affordable homes in the $100,000 range.

For singles and young couples who qualify, Daytona offers job opportunities at places such as Halifax Hospital and surrounding medical offices. Both Daytona State College and Embry Riddle College are large local employers as well. Retail positions are often available at the Volusia Mall and a variety of other businesses in the heart of downtown too.

Daytona is certainly an area that seeks to cultivate its tourist appeal. Many residents love this aspect of living here because there is so much to do throughout the entire area. In addition to 23 miles of local beach access, there are always scores of places to visit and things to see around the Daytona Beach area.

Just a few of the places enjoyed by local residents include: Cypress Aquatic Center, Daytona Beach Pier, the Downtown Farmer's Market, charter fishing excursions, a marine science center, quaint small towns nearby and many area historical attractions.

Fishing and outdoor activities (especially watersports) are always popular here. There are also some very nice local golf courses. Many residents simply enjoy exploring a few of the city's nature trials, while others attend regular concerts or visit places such as Angell & Phelps Chocolate Factory for their free tour.

If you're attracted to a beach town that offers lots of activity and a constant stream of things to do then Daytona Beach should be on the list. It's easy to have fun in this place if you like to mingle with lots of other people from around the country … and even the world. The city tries very hard to attract its guests and residents need to be aware of that.

Car racing, biker events and nightlife are certainly mainstays in this place. But residents who choose this place to live get to see and experience lots of other things that make this area a great place to live. Plus, where else can a family park their car directly on the beach before strolling down to the water's edge for a warm, but refreshing swim? That's Daytona Beach.

Central East Region

DeLand

DeLand is located west of Daytona Beach. Stetson University calls this place home, which gives Deland a "small college town" look and feel.

Its downtown area is lined with antique stores, gift shops and restaurants. Main St. Grill is a favorite lunch destination and Rivertown Antique Mall is also the town's largest building, and it's always full of vintage treasures.

Traveling north out of original part of town will take you to the newer section of DeLand. Here you'll find businesses that include office supply stores, grocery stores and additional types of shopping.

The Deland area is a somewhat unique small town treasure in the state. It doesn't have as many tall palm trees lining the streets as might be seen in other places. Nor does it have a beach just around the corner (although Daytona Beach is a relatively short drive away). But it does have an abundance of crystal clear springs and mossy shade trees throughout its areas.

The average cost of living index number for DeLand is 89.00, compared to the US average of 100. This means that it is somewhat less expensive to live in the area then to live in the average US city. The local real estate is also considered to be affordable as compared to many other markets, with an average listing price of $160,000. There is an even lower median sales price of $95,000. For those who want to shop for homes in a lower price range zip code, 32725 is the least pricey with an average listing price of $168,000.

For retirees who would like to live within a secluded community Cresswind at Victoria Gardens offered homes for sale (in mid-2014) from $100,000 to $400,000. The age restriction for this community is 55+ and both new and resale homes were available.

For parents with children and anyone who enjoys the outdoors, Blue Spring State Part is a destination that can be enjoyed throughout the year. The cold spring waters are home to manatee during the autumn months. These amazing creatures can often be viewed while walking along the springs. The park is so popular on weekends and gets overcrowded so quickly that people sometimes have to be turned away.

Families also enjoy boating, camping, hiking, fishing, scuba diving, snorkeling, swimming and tubing in the Deland area. These are all perks on top of the fact that this city has lower than average living costs. Young professionals, families and retirees all enjoy living in this community.

DeLand is a county seat and its courthouse does provide a few municipal jobs. Larger businesses and most industry-leading companies generally do not call this area "home" however.

Some professionals, however, may not be able to find jobs available within the city in order to advance their careers. They may have to drive to other areas for better paying jobs. Orlando is about an hour's drive away, for example, and there are many job employment opportunities there, especially for professionals.

Deland is considered to be one of Florida's small town gems. Stetson's campus is registered as a National Historic District. Its main street and entire downtown area are filled with quaint gift shops, dining places and lovely walkways to simply enjoy a leisurely stroll.

St. Johns River and beautiful parks surround Deland. The natural beauty of this area is one reason why this town is host to a number of special events each year that include opportunities for residents to explore arts programs, local cultural gatherings, popular lectures and historical displays.

Deland also plays host to one of the largest county fairs in the state each year and is also home to a number of sporting facilities for its residents. There is even a famous skydiving operation in Deland that has been helping customers experience one-in-a-lifetime thrills for over 30 years. It's hard to beat Deland if you're looking for a warm, small town community that also offers lots to do for those who live there.

New Smyrna Beach

New Smyrna Beach is on the east coast of Florida just south of Daytona Beach. Parts of it rest on both the mainland and an adjacent peninsula. Much of its sand features a golden-hue to it and there tends to be less tropical foliage as one gets further from the beach. Its summers are notably hot, with temperatures reaching the 90s and the winter generally features temperatures in the 70s.

New Smyrna Beach has a wonderful, historic, Floridian small town feel. And this is one of its great appeals. Even though it's not too far from crowded Daytona, the beaches here are less crowded and the atmosphere of this place is much more laid back. There are 13 miles of shoreline in New Smyrna beaches, however, and some of these areas are a hotspot for local surfers. Smyrna Inlet, for example, attracts lots of locals and others from neighboring areas, who love riding the waves. In 2009,

New Smyrna Beach was named one of the "best surf towns" by Surfer Magazine. Residents also enjoy New Smyrna Beach for its kitesurfing, swimming, boating, sailing, charter fishing and scuba diving. These are all probably reasons why readers of the Orlando Sentinel newspaper voted

Central East Region

New Smyrna "Best Beach" in 207, 2008, 2009, 2010, 2011, 2012, and 2013.

The old part of this town is lined with gift shops, cafes and older buildings having an "old-shack" look to them that are now home to restaurants. The downtown area is a go-to place for shopping and dining.

The average cost of living in New Smyrna Beach is rated 106.30 compared to the US average of 100. This means that the cost of living is somewhat higher than the average US city. As of mid-2014 the area had hundreds of homes for sale. The average listing price was $289,000 and the median sales price was $161,000. The least expensive zip code in the area was 32725, with an average listing price of $168,000.

The public high school - New Smyrna Beach High - offers something called "Career Academy." This is a program that includes curriculum to prepare students for college with emphasis towards a specific career. The Academy also has partnerships with local businesses that help give students hands on experience with field studies and career shadowing opportunities.

Professionals and others considering a move to this area may have to consider the possibility of working in outlying areas such as Daytona Beach and Orlando. Daytona Beach, for example, offers many more publicly listed job opportunities than New Smyrna Beach. These include positions in sales, healthcare, customer service and skilled labor jobs.

Location is a very attractive feature about New Smyrna Beach. Its location contributes to both its local economy and lifestyle. The Canaveral National Seashore lies just south of New Smyrna and features additional places to go hiking, fishing, swimming and bird watching.

There is a lot to see throughout the whole area, including many local historic and cultural sites. New Smyrna Beach is a place for anyone looking to live in a beautiful, but quieter beach community. It's a charming town where residents enjoy annual events such as the "Shrimp and Seafood Festival."   Here, downtown area restaurants compete for the title, "favorite restaurant".   It's the sort of thing that attracts those who consider this a great place to live.

Central East Region

City of Cape Canaveral

Cape Canaveral is famously home to the Cape Canaveral Air Force Station and NASA's Kennedy Space Center. Cape Canaveral Air Force Station launched the first US earth satellite, the first US spacecraft and the first US astronaut and is responsible for the first moon landing.

It sits on the East Coast of Florida features beautiful white beaches and a flat horizon. There is also a scatter of islands just offshore the Cape. It is these islands that make up the southern portion of a barrier island chain, which are separated from the mainland by Banana River, Indian River and Merritt Island.

Cape Canaveral, in one sense, certainly has an aura of the typical Florida beach town. Palm trees and tropical plants make up the foliage, a statue of a manatee sits at the local riverside park and beachgoers enjoy the ocean in true Floridian fashion, with lots of boogie boards and floats in view. But it is very much a place to live, work and play. It's a very busy place, with lots of activities, industries and home choices. There is something for everyone here.

Cape Canaveral's average cost of living is 98.5 compared to the US average of 100. This means that it is generally less expensive to live in Cape Canaveral than the average city. As of mid-2014 the area saw a decrease in the average listing price of a home by 5.0%. This brought the average listing to $230,000. The median sales price also saw a drop of 11.2% and was at $137,000.

At the time of this writing, however, all of the area's most popular neighborhoods saw an increase in average listing prices for homes. The most an expensive of the popular neighborhoods is Columbiad Plaza with an average listing of just under $90,000. The most expensive of the popular neighborhoods in the area was Port View Townhomes with an average listing of just under $575,000.

Cape Canaveral's job opportunities also include those of neighboring Melbourne, Florida. As of mid-2014 the surrounding areas had hundreds of job openings. These included sales, healthcare, customer service and engineering. There is a diverse business climate here that also includes retail companies, aerospace firms and high-tech corporations. And there are also a variety of tourism and convention businesses.

Nearby Port Canaveral is a busy place for both shipping and the luxury cruise industry. Ships are constantly arriving and departing to the area.

Cape Canaveral itself does not have any major retirement communities for those who would like to live in one, but it does have fairly reasonable real estate prices; some are even ender under $100,000. These lower real estate prices and lower than average cost of living would be helpful to anyone moving to the area, especially young families and retirees living on a budget.

The Cape Canaveral area is home to a diverse population. Many residents are affiliated with one of the large number of area churches that are part of most communities. And the public school system is considered to be one of the better ones in the State. There are also numerous private schooling options too.

Cape Canaveral is a thriving Florida beachside community that is still considered to be affordable by most residents. It offers many good paying jobs to qualified applicants and continues to be a magnet for companies that wish to grow in a "business friendly" environment.

There is a great local library, a well-developed artisan community and outdoor/watersports association to match just about any interest. Residents can also participate in activities such as racquetball, shuffleboard, tennis, biking and flag-football. Events and gatherings of all types are commonplace.

Locals generally get to enjoy the benefits of living in this tourist town. A large number of establishments offer shopping, dining and fun activities on a daily basis. All of these combine to help make this city a great place to live for individuals of all ages.

Central East Region

Melbourne

Melbourne, Florida is located east of Interstate 95 and has parts that are both mainland and peninsula. It is only about an hour away from Kennedy Space Center in Cape Canaveral and an hour away from Disney World in Orlando.

Most of Melbourne is mainland, but a small piece of it is located on the barrier island that sits between the mainland and the Atlantic Ocean. One bridge crosses the Indian River Lagoon separating the two.

The area has been growing at a slow rate and is still considered to be a small town. It's approximately 40 square miles with an estimated population of over 75,000. One of the largest area employers is the city itself which gives jobs to more than 800 employees.

Professionals who might consider moving to the area also can look for work in nearby Orlando. This helps add more options to job opportunities. Orlando is such a large city that it has over 2,500 jobs available as of mid-2014.

Melbourne's Florida average cost-of-living is 89.40 compared to the national average of 100. This lower cost of living would be very appealing to anyone that moves here, especially young adults and those with young families.

Central East Region

In the Melbourne area there were nearly 1,000 homes for sale with an average listing price of just under $250,000 as of mid-2014. The median sales price was $146,000. Although those prices might be a bit steep for some folks, the large number of homes available throughout Melbourne gave them a better chance to find something that fit their price range.

People often choose to live in Melbourne because of its lower living costs, its close proximity to Orlando (and other urban areas) and its quiet beaches. It's a less pricey Florida beach town with quick access to larger urban amenities. And when residents want to stretch their legs, they often do so by at Melbourne's beautiful Pineapple Part, on the Indian River Lagoon, or by visiting a nearby attraction, such as Cape Canaveral.

Local residents love taking advantage of all the things you'd expect from a beach town. There is an abundance of boating, fishing, swimming and snorkeling. But golfing is also popular throughout this area.

Professionals and other residents often enjoy working in Orlando and then coming home to a more laid back atmosphere away from the city. Melbourne isn't considered to be a major employment area, although it is considered to be a small hub for certain high tech businesses and also a place for educational and medical services. (Much of the high-tech industry is located near Melbourne's international airport).

Melbourne has an historic downtown area, filled with small shops and restaurants. And there is also a local arts district that offers regular activities, including cultural and educational events.

Many retirees throughout the area certainly appreciate its lower than average living costs, as they spend days relaxing in the sand and watching dolphins swim by. For parents with active children the immediate area may not necessarily offer as much in the way of local events or attractions that some towns do. But Walt Disney World is just an hour away, as is the famous Wet N' Wild Water Park and Islands of Adventure park. These are many of the reasons why Melbourne is considered by many to be one of Florida's top places to live.

Southwest Region

The greater Naples area is located on the west side of Florida. It is several hours south of Tampa and is almost directly across from Miami, which is located on the east coast of the state. Naples itself is one of the wealthiest cities in the nation. It has the second densest population of millionaires per capita and the sixth highest per capita income in the US.

In the late 1800s John Stuart Williams, a former Confederate general and Kentucky senator, founded Naples, Florida. It got its name from its large bay that people described as larger than that of the popular Italian city of Naples, Italy. Magazines and newspapers would publish stories about the area's abundant fish and lovely weather. They frequently talked about a few similar characteristics shared with the famous Italian peninsula.

In 1927 an extension of the railroad linked Miami to Naples. Later, after the Great Depression and the end of World War II, people began making their way to the area. After a hurricane hit in the 1940s a dredging company helped clean up the area, widened the Jamaica Channel and created a subdivision called "Aqualane Shores". As new channels were added and dredging continued, Naples residents were able to do more construction to improve the city. Distinct features of Naples include canals that give many homeowners waterfront property and access to the Gulf of Mexico.

Naples' economy is largely tourism based. It was once driven by agriculture and real estate, but as the growth of those two industries subsided the economy depended much more on tourism. Today the top employers in the area are the public school districts, NCH Healthcare System, the Home Depot and the Ritz Carlton.

As Naples built a name for itself, the city of Cape Coral also began to develop. Just like in Naples, Cape Coral construction companies dug canals and developed neighborhoods with waterfront properties. The first homes were completed in

1958. As word about Naples got out, celebrities also began showing interest in Cape Coral.

At first, Cape Coral was home to many retirees, but during the 1990s many professionals and younger families started coming to the area. Today, about 20% of Cape Coral's residence are seasonal and come to town to visit their vacation homes and escape the cold northern winters.

The greater Naples area has hundreds of miles of canals -- more than any other place in the world. There are so many of them that the water's tides have compensated for them and not naturally rise and fall in the same way they once did.

Nearly every day in the greater Naples area feels like summer. There are approximately 355 days with lots of sunshine every year. Summers are rainy, however, and feature occasional showers at some point about 145 days each year. The weather is warm and humid with highs in the 90s. A December record low was once recorded at 24°F, but on average the winter weather does not drop below the mid-60s.

People especially love Naples for its beaches. Gulf Shore Boulevard runs next to Lowdermilk Beach, a popular family beach in the Naples vicinity. Naples Beach is the most well-known in the area. It has over 10 miles of beautiful white sand and a 1,000 foot long fishing pier. This beach is a very full during heavy tourist inflows so some locals will sneak up to Vanderbilt Beach just North of the area.

The pride of Naples is its deep-sea fishing. Prized catches are caught every year. The Snook fishing is said to be some of the best in Florida (the record for the area is 36 pounds at the time of this writing). These big fish can be caught year-round.

Fisherman in the Southwest region of Florida also eagerly wait for the perfect time of year (May through July) to catch Tarpon. They are caught by fly-fishing in the still waters of the canals. Redfish are a smaller year-round catch. They live in the mangroves and oyster beds. The average size of a redfish is 25-35 lbs. And Sea Trout are another year-round favorite to catch; they are generally smaller at around 20-25 lbs.

Perhaps the most exciting catches for some fishermen in Southwest Florida are sharks. The warm months bring bull sharks, lemon sharks and black tipped sharks to area waters. The biggest catches generally weigh over 300 pounds and some of these fish are 9+ feet long. Many residents and tourists hire one of the local charter boats to take them fishing for sharks in local waters. Teenagers and young kids especially like coming to watch these animals be pulled up onto a boat and then re-released.

Cape Coral, Pine Island, Bonita Springs, Punta Gorda, Fort Myers and Naples are all part of the southwest of Florida. These neighboring cities and towns all offer their unique brand of a Floridian life. Some emphasize quiet settings, while others showcase sunny beaches and others proudly display their intertwining canals with adjacent properties. Aside from the southern Florida Keys, this region truly features some of the best tropical areas within the entire state.

Southwest Region

Fort Myers

Fort Myers is located on the west coast of Florida, south of Punta Gorda and on the east side of Lochmoor Waterway directly across from Cape Coral. It is one of the two major cities in the Southwest region of the state. Like its neighboring city to the north, Punta Gorda, it has many neighborhoods where homeowners have access to the water. The land layout looks somewhat like Venice, California in that many homeowners have a yard where they can reach water.

Most waterways within Fort Myers itself tend to be dark and murky and because the city isn't directly on the Gulf. Fort Myers beach, directly across from Sanibel Island, is quite nice, however. The general area reflects a tropical south Florida vibe with lots of royal palms and warm weather throughout the year.

Fort Myers has quite an array of activities. Its River District has a weekly farmers market, a regular music walk and art walk and an annual Artfest. Golfing is especially big in this area, especially at Eastwood Golf Course, which is been open since 1886.

Ice skating classes, hockey games, soccer games and volleyball games can all be found at the Skatium & Fitness Center. (Who would have thought one could play ice hockey in Florida?) And both residents and tourists alike frequently escape hot days by cooling off with a visit the Fort Myers Museum of History located downtown.

The average cost of living is rated at 94.10 which is lower than the US average of 100. The area's real estate market experienced a decrease as of mid-2014. The average listing price for a home dropped 6.8% to $305,000. The median sales price saw a drastic decrease of 42.5% for a current average of $79,000. There are many homes in the area in a variety of price ranges.

As of mid-2014 the Fort Myers area had hundreds of job openings for those who qualify. These included sales opportunities, customer service, healthcare career openings and management positions. Verizon Wireless and the US Army were the top employers in the area at the time.

Those moving to the area with children may take note that Coronado High School, Edison Park Creative on Cleveland Avenue and Expressive Arts School on Euclid Ave are the two top rated schools in Fort Myers. There are always other schooling options, including home schooling, which is a popular alternative to public education all throughout Florida.

Resident singles, couples, families with children and retirees all appreciate the lower than average cost of living here in Fort Myers. The area's many attractions and activities, which help make it a popular tourist destination, are frequently enjoyed by those who live here.

The general look and feel of Fort Myers is that of a true Florida resort town. There are a seemingly endless number of attractions that cater primarily to tourists. But this, ironically, is part of what attracts many people to move here. In short, Fort Myers is simply a fun, happening place.

The area surrounding Fort Myers is teeming with diverse things to do or see on any given day. It would be possible to go skating in the morning, then enjoy lunch at one of the many eateries near the beach, and then visit an Alligator farm later in the afternoon, and then watch the sun set over the Gulf of Mexico in the evening. If you don't mind the constant stream of visiting tourists that come here each year then Fort Myers is a great place to live for those attracted to an active Floridian lifestyle.

Southwest Region

Cape Coral

Cape Coral is the largest city between Miami and Tampa, with an estimated population of 650,000 people. The city is situation on a large Peninsula, at the Gulf of Mexico, just under Fort Myers. Its nickname is "Waterfront Wonderland" because of its 400 miles of waterways. In fact, it has more canals than any other city in the world.

Days filled with sunshine are quite frequent here, with about 355 days per year featuring lots of sun throughout the year. Winters are generally very mild, and summers typically bring lots of heat, humidity, rainy afternoons and temperatures in the 90s.

Real estate in Cape Coral varies depending on the zip code. The average listing price for the area is $430,000. The median sales price is $225,000; which an 8.3% increase at the beginning of 2014. It's least expensive popular zip codes is 33909 with an average listing price of $370,000. Its most expensive zip code is 33914 with an average listing price of $430,000.

The area's average cost of living index was rated at 96.40, compared to the national average of 100. This means that it is somewhat less expensive to live in Cape Coral in the average US city. Its economy is based primarily on government services, retail, real estate and healthcare. Its job opportunities frequently include sales, healthcare, management, retail and customer service positions.

Those with children looking to move to the area will find Ida S. Baker High School, located within Cape Coral on Agualinda Boulevard, as a top-rated public school. And Oasis Charter Elementary School and Providence Christian School are considered to be among the best elementary schools in the area.

There tends to be a lot of local events for children each year. Some of the best ones include summer camps at the William Austin Youth center. Cape Coral is well-known for featuring several concerts throughout the year for its adult population too.

Many residents live a very energetic lifestyle that includes lots of outdoor activity. Among Cape Corals most exciting events and activities are those connected with popular water sports. There is lots of waterskiing, boating, fishing and diving all throughout the area.

Fishing is especially popular in Cape Coral. The fishing here includes everything from pier fishing with a buddy, to paddling a small kayak on a man-made freshwater canal in order to cast a line, to paying the captain of a local deep-sea charter to help you reel in an ocean catch.

Charter boats are frequently rented so both residents and area visitors can experience a day out on the Gulf while trying to land some big fish. Deep-sea fishing in the area includes snapper, king fish, barracuda and tuna. Coastal fishing is particularly better here than most of Florida because of the nearby mangrove preserve, which creates a wonderful habitat that supports local wildlife.

Cape Coral's lower than average cost of living somewhat offsets its generally high real estate prices. It's also a better place for working residents to find a job, especially professionals and skilled workers of all kinds.

Cape Coral is very much purposed to be a "waterfront community." If the idea of living in a city with canals, boating, fishing and watersports on the Gulf of Mexico appeals to you then you're definitely going to want to consider Cape Coral. There are many other outdoor activities available to locals, of course, but those who have a love for the water are often drawn here.

The area is an active, family-friendly place; there are lots of events and activities taking place year-round for every member of the family, including children. This is why many singles, couples, families with children and retirees call this place home.

Pine Island

Pine Island is the largest island in the state of Florida. It is located on the Gulf of Mexico just west of Fort Myers. The Matlacha Pass passes between the island and the mainland. This barrier island is also west of Cape Coral. It features beautiful Gulf beaches while being surrounded by mangroves and three aquatic preserves.

The island is home to four unofficial towns: St. James City, Bokeelia, Pine Island Center and Pineland. These are all smaller communities within Pine Island.

The wildlife refuges around Pine Island include the Matlacha Pass National Wildlife Refuge and Little Pine Island. They're home to egrets, ibises, ospreys and spoonbills, which are all enjoyed by sightseers and nature lovers throughout the year.

Many of its neighborhoods give residents water access … many directly from their own backyards. A large percentage of Pine Island residents own boats and spend lots of their free time on the water.

Events on the island include charity golf tournaments, fishing tournaments, boat parades along the west coast and seafood festivals. Of course, the main appeal of Pine Island is its water sports. Locals regularly enjoy swimming, paddle-boarding, canoeing, water-skiing and, of course, fishing. The fishing around Pine Island is said to be among of the very best in Florida.

The coral rock on Pine Island is ideal for lychee and mango trees which grown throughout the island. Tourists have been known to travel more than 100 miles just to purchase some of its homegrown fruit.

The area's average cost of living is 166.60 out of a US average of 100. It's significantly more expensive to live here than the average US city. Its real estate market, as of mid-2014, also had very few homes available. Home prices at this time averaged between $200,000 and $500,000.

Real estate types vary just a bit. There are waterfront homes, off-water homes and condominiums. The price range for an average waterfront home is $600,000 to $800,000. And off-water homes average half that, at about $300,000-$400,000.

Schools servicing Pine Island include Fox Chapel Middle School and Wider Horizons School. Both are late located in Spring Hill.

Many residents view Pine Island as a "little corner of Paradise." Even though it's only about a 30 minute drive from busy Fort Myers, the tranquil, rural setting of Pine Island seems like a world away from any nearby hustle and bustle.

Both locals and visitors love Pine Island for its beauty, natural settings and wildlife. All sorts of nature lovers, including hikers, kayakers-canoers and bird watchers find something to really like about this place.

This isn't really the place to come in order to find work. There are a few job openings occasionally, often in the areas of retail, customer service and sales.

Pine Island is sort of a mix between a small town (with some residences), a fishing/boating community, a nature preserve and an eclectic group of family-owned shops and assorted small businesses. It's apparent this is a premier and exclusive community. But those who can afford to live on Pine Island say it's well worth it.

Punta Gorda

Punta Gorda is located on the west coast of Florida, in between Sarasota and Fort Myers. The Charlotte Harbor runs along its northern and western side. Punta Gorda is on the mainland, with Charlotte Harbor and clusters of small islands between it and the Gulf of Mexico.

The area's neighborhood streets look almost like weaving islands. The layout of Punta Gorda somewhat resembles the famous neighborhoods in Venice, California. The dark blue waters of Charlotte Harbor, which surrounding the city are warm and inviting. Much of the city's shores are liberally covered with royal palm trees everywhere the eye can see.

Certain sections of Punta Gorda definitely have the look and feel of "old Florida" to them. You can see old-fashioned tin roofs on many buildings, some houses features lovely wide verandas and there are even a few brick lanes and decades old street lamps in some places.

Punta Gorda has 4 public schools in the area. They are Charlotte High School, Sallie Jones Elementary School, Punta Gorda Middle School and the Charlotte County Florida Southwestern State College campus. These are all located within the city.

Southwest Region

This sub-tropical city often projects the warm, humid weather one might expect from this part of Florida. It's been hit pretty hard by a couple of hurricanes too. It suffered a lot of destruction from Hurricane Charlie in 2004 and damage from Hurricane Donna back in the 60s. Since then the area has mostly dodged a few other big storms. Most locals know the "hurricane drill" though. Evacuation warnings are well understood by residents who've lived here awhile.

The average cost of living is only slightly higher than the US average of 100. It is 101.60, meaning that it is very close to the national average. Punta Gorda's average listing price for a home is just shy of $270,000. Its median sales price is $165,000. For those who are looking to spend under $200,000 the area has three zip codes that are appealing to many buyers. The first one is area code 33952 with an average listing price of just under $160,000. The second is 33948 with an average listing price of just under $175,000. Lastly there is 33983 with an average listing price of $170,000.

Career opportunities for those living in Punta Gorda may also include those in Fort Myers, as many residents drive south to work in the Fort Myers area. As of mid-2014 there were hundreds of locally advertised job openings. For those who qualify the positions included sales, healthcare, nursing, management and customer service.

Many local events around Punta Gorda tend to be low key. It's a beautiful, yet quiet place to live most of the time. (It very much has the feel of a small town). Pottery classes are frequently held at the Arts Center downtown, yoga classes are often conducted on the beachside and art shows commonly take place in the midst of picturesque streets.

Most people enjoy the waterfront shopping at places like Harborwalk and Fisherman's Village on Charlotte Harbor. And history lovers can visit picturesque small museums such as A.C. Freeman House, which features authentic Victorian period furniture. But if you do visit here then don't miss the Farmer's Market, which was recently voted "best in Florida." The market features fresh fruits and vegetables, to be sure, but also a huge variety of organic and ethnic specialty foods.

Punta Gorda is a charming town with interesting neighborhoods. Many homeowners access to the water from their properties. Young adults, families and retirees all enjoy this place. And for those who are career minded, Punta Gorda and to the Fort Myers area offer a good selection of job opportunities.

Bonita Springs

Bonita Springs is located on the southwest coast of Florida and is a part of both the Cape Coral and the Fort Myers area. It is located on a barrier island, with Estero Bay to the east of it and the Gulf of Mexico to the west.

The sands in and around Bonita Springs change slightly down its coastline, as sugar-white beaches frequently turn into sands reflecting off-white hues. The area is scattered with beautiful royal palms trees. These palms are not common in northern and central Florida and add to the area's beautiful tropical scenery.

When traveling south along Florida's west coast Bonita Springs is one of the first cities you would reach that features a true tropical climate. Its neighboring city to the north, Fort Myers Beach, is the cutoff point for "subtropical" climate in the state.

The average cost of living index in Bonita Springs is 117.20 compared to the US average of 100. This means that it is slightly more expensive to live in this place than in the average US city. Bonita Springs has a more expensive real estate market for those who want to spend under $250,000 for a home. The city is full of beautiful Spanish styled homes painted with whites, creams and corals. Most yards have shady palm trees in the front and some have an occasional coquina rock adorning the yard.

The average listing price as of 2014 was a little over $635,000. The median sales price was listed as being a little over $250,000. The least expensive zip code is 33904 with an average listing price of $330,000.

For families with children the highest-rated school in the area is Gospel Baptist Christian School, located on Old 41 Road. It's a private school, of course. There certainly public schools in the area, including Bonita Springs Elementary School and Bonita Springs Charter School. All of these are located within the Lee County Public Schools district.

As of mid-2014 job opportunities in the Bonita Springs area consisted of few available positions. The ones advertised included openings in management, sales, healthcare and customer service.

The two companies with the most available positions at this time were Rural King (a hardware store) and Hertz. In other words, Bonita Springs itself isn't a place many job seekers target for employment. This is important for those who will need to find employment after moving to Florida strongly need to consider. One thing to note, however, is that civil leaders in Bonita Springs are actively trying to attract more businesses. They particularly emphasize the lower taxes and lower costs of commercial retail spaces that are available here.

Bonita Springs is ideal for the retiree who wants to live on an island and enjoy Florida's version of sub-tropical weather throughout the year. It's simply a beautiful place to live for those with bigger budgets who can afford it.

Younger adults and families with children are certainly found here. But they tend to be successful professionals and business owners who can afford the higher cost of living. Bonita Springs isn't known for being a place that offers abundant job opportunities for unskilled workers.

Bonita Springs' main appeal is its small-town feel, uncrowded beaches and tropical island-like lifestyle. A day in the life of a resident might include a leisurely morning walk on the beach and lunch at Pincher's Crab Shack on Bonita Crossings Boulevard. That could be followed up with some swimming in wonderfully warm Gulf waters (water temperatures are often in the 80s many months of the year).

Residents looking for things to do can certainly find community events and exhibitions on the public calendar. But the most advertised things to do here will most likely be associated with one of the many parks, wildlife sanctuaries or nature programs in the area. Nature ... nature ... and more nature ... for nature/beach lovers.

Not much gets in the way of a quiet day for most residents here. Individuals seem to earnestly pursue the activities of strolling along the shore or lounging on a beach with purposeful intent.

Naples

Naples is known as being one of the wealthiest cities in the nation. It has the sixth highest income per capita in the US. It also has the second-highest density of millionaires per capita. Being that it is one of the wealthiest cities it is no surprise that its homes are some of the most expensive in the country as well. Some properties are listed for well over $40 million.

It's not surprising many people flock to Naples. It has gorgeous beaches to go along with year-round sub-tropical temperatures. Beach sands are mostly pearl-white and lined with tall palm trees and sea grass.

The majority of public events and activities in Napes seem to reflect a love of the water. Thanks to regularly great weather and long summers, locals can enjoy boating, windsurfing, jet skiing and sailing year-round.

For those who love to fish, the area around Naples is known for offering big catches at times. Tarpon, grouper, pompano and sea trout can usually be found in abundance. And anyone who doesn't own their own boat can always charter one for deep-sea fishing and shelling adventure. Anglers who prefer staying on dry land can enjoy the newly remodeled Naples pier, which has

1,000 feet reserved for those who'd like to cast a line over the side in order to catch something.

Golfing is also hugely popular here. Visitors regularly come from all over the US to play the golf courses in and around the Naples area.

One other thing to note about Naples is its proximity to the Everglades. The glades can be reached with a relatively short drive from any part of Naples. This means just about any Everglades activity or program is easily accessible from Naples, including alligator farms and shows.

Naples' average listing price is quite steep at $820,000, as of mid-2014. The median sales price is much lower at just under $250,000. One of its most popular neighborhoods is Royal Harbor with an average listing price of $1.2 million dollars. The most expensive popular neighborhoods is Port Royal with home selling on average for about $11 million dollars.

For those considering moving to the area with children, the Lorenzo Walker Institute of Technology is a top-rated High School located on Estey Avenue. Parkside Elementary School is the local public elementary school, but those who prefer to send their children to a private school can check out the Naples Christian Academy located on Santa Barbara Ave.

Southwest Region

The average cost of living index in Naples is 189.60 compared to the national average of 100. This means that it is almost twice as expensive to live in the area as compared to the average US city. Naples has a pretty strong job market. There are typically hundreds of job openings for those who qualify. These include positions in information technology, healthcare, management, customer service and sales.

Retirees who would like to move to Naples but don't want to invest in a home can choose from several retirement communities in the area. The best known are VI at Bentley Village, located on Village Circle, the Lely Palms Retirement Community and the Harbor Chase Memory Village.

Naples is considered by many to be the "crown jewel" of southwest Florida. It offers an abundance of natural attractions and sophisticated elegance with a spoonful of old Florida charm mixed in. There is always something for the eye to behold, including natural vistas and man-made architecture.

Locals love Naples for its beaches, year-round water sports, fishing, shopping and wonderful foods. There is an abundance of fun here, especially as it pertains to outdoor activity. But it all does come with a healthy price-tag. Naples is often a playground for wealthy property owners and visitors. While one doesn't need to be rich to live here, they must be prepared to "pay more in order to play more."

Southeast Region

Southeast Florida, also known as the Miami metropolitan area, contains some of the most popular places to live in Florida. The cities in this region include Miami, Hollywood, Fort Lauderdale, Pompano Beach, West Palm Beach, Miami Beach, Boca Raton, Deerfield Beach, Delray Beach, Boynton Beach, Pembroke Pines, Plantation, Port St. Lucie and Homestead.

The climate of this part of Florida falls under the category of "tropical monsoon climate." Between May and October the wet season brings hot, humid days, with thunderstorms regularly occurring in late afternoons. This is when the hurricane season takes place.

Southeast Region

The dry season lasts from October until April. During this period, it's not uncommon for residential areas to be placed under water restrictions by officials. There are also regular warnings issued to help residents be careful about the possibility of brushfires. Every once in a while a cold front will come through and drop temperatures into the 60s, but generally the Miami area experiences what most people would consider to be a year-round summer, with temperatures regularly in the 80s and 90s.

Officially, hurricane season runs from June 1st to November 30th. If the Miami area were to be directly hit by a hurricane then the most likely time that would happen would be during Cape Verde season, which begins in mid-August. The Cape Verde is a type of hurricane that forms near the Cape Verde Islands. These are the largest and most dangerous storms of the hurricane season.

Miami itself was first claimed for Spain during a Spanish mission conducted in 1567. It wasn't until 1821 that Miami, with the rest of Florida, was ceded to the US. A local citrus grower named Julia Tuttle is known as the only woman to ever conceive a major city in the US. It was her crops that brought attention to what would eventually be called "one of the finest building sites in Florida".

Southeast Region

The end of the Florida land boom in the 1920s and the Great Depression were two events during the 20th century that temporarily stunted the growth of Miami area. But during World War II, Miami was a base for US defense against German submarines. That activity helped spark an increase in population throughout the entire region. The whole area has continued growing in population ever since.

In 1959, an influx of Cubans seeking refuge from Fidel Castro came to Miami, adding even more to the population. The 1980s and 1990s were especially high periods of growth due to continuing immigration.

By the time the year 2000 rolled around, Miami was becoming a major financial center in the South. It now features the densest number of banks of any city in America. In the space of a century, Miami has gone from being home to just 1,000 residents to nearly 5.3 million. This is one reason why it is sometimes called the "Magic City."

As the heart of the southeast region today, Miami is a world leader in finance, commerce and international business. It's such an influential city in the global marketplace that it has been named an "Alpha Minus World City," meaning one of the most important economic places in the world's economy.

Several large companies have their headquarters in the Miami area. These include: US Century Bank, Vector Group, Norwegian Cruise Lines, Royal Caribbean Cruise Lines, Celebrity Cruises, Carnival Corporation and Burger King.

The greater Miami area is also a major television center. It specializes in Spanish-language media. It is also a major location for recording music and is home to Sony Music Latin as well as many other smaller labels.

The city of Miami's skyline includes 50 skyscrapers. During the previous real estate boom there were 100 high-rise construction projects approved, but the market crash of 2008 put an end to many of those projects as the area headed into recession. During this time, like the rest of the country, many Miami residents and investors were affected by the real estate crash. The economy of the entire region suffered as the area ranked 8th in foreclosures within the US.

At the time of this writing, the city has largely bounced back economically. Its two international ports are two of the nation's busiest. Not only does cargo go to and from this place, Miami is also host to the world's busiest cruising port.

Southeast Region

In addition to finance and business, tourism is an important industry throughout the entire Southeast region of the state. Miami alone welcomes nearly 40 million visitors a year and these tourists spend over $17 billion dollars in Florida. Visitors often come to this area in order to visit its popular beaches and experience its glamorous nightclubs. But most local residents simply enjoy the vibrant culture and diverse economic-employment opportunities that promise to enhance their lives.

Southeast Florida has a unique look and feel apart from other regions of the state. Its tropical weather, ethnic diversity, broad cultural influences, culinary flavors and financial incentives draw people here from all over the world.

Southeast Region

Boca Raton

Boca Raton is on the east coast of southern Florida within the Palm Beach County. It has a tropical rain forest climate with summer average highs in the 90s and winter average highs in the 70s.

Boca Raton – more commonly known as simply "Boca" – has attracted both residents and tourists since the 1950s. The name is derived from the Spanish phrase "Boca de Ratones," which has been translated to mean "a shallow inlet of sharp-pointed rocks which scrapes a ship's cables."

There are many reasons why people love living in and visiting Boca. But one thing in particular that is a draw to many individuals is Boca's beaches along the Atlantic shore and the unique snorkeling environment that exists here.

Snorkelers are able to visit natural reefs within a relatively short distance from the shoreline. Having these reefs so accessible means that it's possible to go from lounging on the beach to a swimming along an amazing coral habitat without having to jump in a boat to get there.

Boca's beaches and channels reflect beautiful hues of blues and greens and the waters here are clear enough for swimmers to really do some sightseeing under water as they snorkel and dive along the beaches. Royal palm trees and sea grasses create an additional backdrop that make for a picture-postcard tropical look and feel.

The average cost of living in Boca Raton is 118.10 compared to a US average of 100. This means that the area is significantly more expensive to live in than the average US city. As of mid-2014, Boca Raton's real estate market was very active. There were nearly as many homes recently sold as there were total homes for sale. The average listing price was $755,000, but the median sales price was substantially lower at $260,000. The most affordable home prices were located in zip code 33411 and had an average price of $297,000. The most expensive zip code was 33480, with an average listing price of over $2 million.

Office Depot is a major employer in the area with a 28-acre facility within the city. But many of Boca's job opportunities also come from neighboring Fort Lauderdale. These include insurance positions, management opportunities, customer service jobs, healthcare careers and sales/marketing opportunities.

Much of Boca Raton's economy is related to tourism and includes many wealthy visitors who lavishly spend on real estate, entertainment and personal accessories. Many of Boca Raton's events, therefore, cater to this particular group of tourists. As a result, it's not uncommon to a see annual, high-end car and boat shows come to town. The Concours d' Elegance, for example, is one of the most anticipated car shows every year that even attracts certain car loving celebrities such as Jay Leno.

All of these things contribute to making Boca a premier place to live as well as a vacation spot. The city includes art museums, art festivals, concerts, specifically themed clubs and nightlife, specialty shops and boutiques, elite stores and extraordinary restaurants. It features sports, including golfing and every sort of outdoor activity imaginable. If one can afford living here there are an endless number of things to do and see.

Those who do choose to move to this beautiful tropical city typically desire upscale lifestyle, rich cultural atmosphere, beautiful beaches, offshore diving and year-round activities and events. Boca delivers on them all.

Fort Lauderdale

Fort Lauderdale is on the southeastern Atlantic coast of Florida, south of Boca Raton and north of Miami. Its average year-round temperatures are in the mid-70s making it a popular tourist destination. The greater Fort Lauderdale area has over 12 million visitors every year. And cruise ships sail in and out of Fort Lauderdale's Port Everglades year-round.

During the wet season locals know that afternoon thunderstorms are almost a guarantee. They pass through the same time every day. During the dry season, November through April, there are occasional cold fronts, but daytime temperatures rarely drop below the 60s.

The 7 miles of beaches at the edge of the city are the main attraction and are much loved by locals and visitors alike. A unique architectural structure called the "wavewall" runs parallel to the beach and there is a famous promenade that features a huge array of shops, cafes, restaurants and entertainment venues of all sorts. On most days beach activities include swimming, snorkeling, kayaking, scuba diving, windsurfing, fishing and rollerblading along the shoreline.

Fort Lauderdale is often referred to as "The Venice of America" because it features nearly 165 miles of canals. These canals, constructed during the1920s, provide extensive mobility for large numbers of boats to operate within the city itself. There are now companies that offer gondola rides to passengers in canopied boats using quiet electric motors. It's a wonderful, leisurely way to see unique sights along the banks.

The average cost of living in Fort Lauderdale is 118.40 compared to the national average of 100. This means that it is significantly more expensive to live in Fort Lauderdale than the average US city. The average real estate listing price in the area, as of mid-2014, was $852,000. The median sales price was somewhat lower at $310,000. The most expensive of the most popular neighborhoods in the area was Central Beach, with an average listing price of over $1 million. The most affordable of the most popular neighborhoods was Imperial Point, with an average listing price of a little over $300,000.

Because of its close proximity to its neighboring cities job opportunities include those in Miami, Boca Raton, and Hollywood Florida. On average there are always lots of advertised jobs throughout the area to qualified candidates. The Fort Lauderdale job market includes sales opportunities, customer service positions, healthcare openings and management jobs.

One unique field of work in the area centers on boating. Boating is a cottage industry in Fort Lauderdale and much of the work relates to boatbuilding and maintenance. Thousands of people are employed in the boating industry throughout the city. It's not hard to understand why either, since this place hosts over 100 marinas with over 42,000 yachts in residence.

Anyone moving here needs to know that the population in Fort Lauderdale swells during the winter months. Thousands of "snow birds" from northern states temporarily take refuge from the cold throughout the area. Many residents dislike the extra traffic in the streets. But they also recognize that such visitors make valuable economic and cultural contributions. Their presence is a part of what makes this city a "happening place."

For those who love staying busy, Fort Lauderdale is a great place to be. There are virtually unlimited recreational, cultural and outdoor opportunities

A few of Fort Lauderdale's major shopping areas include: the Galleria Mall, Festival Flea Market Mall and shops along Las Olas Boulevard. And great food is always available from both local dives and world-class restaurants.

Southeast Region

Singles, couples, retirees and families with children can all be found in great abundance here. It would be best to visit during the winter (the height of snow bird season) to get an accurate sense of whether or not this lively place is a right fit for you. But if you enjoy an active lifestyle with an adequate budget then Fort Lauderdale is certainly worth your attention.

Port St. Lucie

Port St. Lucie is located on the southeastern coast of Florida. As of mid-2014, it had an estimated 165,000 residents and was the ninth largest city in Florida.

This town began many decades ago as a fishing camp. A few farms were also started in the area and it remained this way for a long time. The population began growing throughout the mid-20th century and has continued (albeit at a much slower pace) ever since. The economic recession of 2008 hit the area very hard, but it continues to be a popular vacation spot for tourists.

Port St. Lucie is still very much a beach town, but there is a whole lot more here. Many residents enjoy golfing and many other types of sporting events. The Saint Lucie River attracts simple nature lovers and outdoor enthusiasts alike. (The entire river region is well-known for its natural beauty). It's a great place for hiking, canoeing, kayaking, fishing (and plain ole' swimming), horse riding and guided expeditions.

During cooler months the average temperatures ranges between 60° and 70° and during warmer months, temperatures reach the 80s and 90s. Because of its natural surroundings and location between Miami and Orlando, Port St. Lucie is a popular tourist destination. Residents and visitors alike enjoy its beautiful natural environment and extensive parks system.

Port St. Lucie has both traditional neighborhoods and what is termed "mixed-use" neighborhoods. This means that residential areas often blend with commercial, cultural, institutional, industrial and business spaces.

There are a range of housing types here, including town homes, apartments and single-family homes. Some of it most popular neighborhoods enable residents to walk to nearby retail and dining locations on adjacent streets.

Kids in Port St. Lucie have the opportunity to live in a beach town and be a part of a wider community of opportunities. A few of the better-rated public schools are in this area too. Instead of having traditional zoning rules for schools, Port St. Lucie offers an open enrollment system that lets public-schooling parents choose from a variety of schools within the area they live. This gives parents a little more flexibility with regards to choosing where students might attend in order to pursue their education.

The average cost of living in Port St. Lucie is rated as 92.50 out of the US average of 100. This means it's slightly less expensive to live in the area than the average US city. For those willing to spend over $100,000, the local real estate market is somewhat more affordable. The average listing price of homes throughout the town, as of mid-2014, was $200,000 and the median sales price was $132,000. The least expensive zip code in the area was 34983, with an average listing price of $156,000.

At the time of this writing, there was a large advertised selection of jobs available in Port St. Lucie. These jobs included healthcare opportunities (especially nursing), sales positions, management openings and customer service work. There were also a large variety of commercial hospitality jobs available because of the large tourist industry throughout the area.

Events around Port St. Lucie are often relaxed and family friendly. The Port St. Lucie Botanical Gardens, for example, regularly hosts evenings for adults that include a "Jazz and Blues" night, while children are entertained with butterfly events. Avid gardeners, of course, get to enjoy the sort of plant growing education one might expect from such a place, in addition to the occasional plant sale.

Port St. Lucie's civic center is also a very popular spot. The center plays host to an unending variety of fun and interesting events. These include everything as diverse as comedy, bodybuilding, church socials, business gatherings and everything in between.

Singles, couples, larger families and retirees alike all seem to enjoy living in Port St. Lucie. When one considers the fact that this place offers opportunities for income, relatively uncrowded beaches, wonderful nature preserves, sports activities and many other types of recreation then it becomes even clearer why many people choose to move here.

Southeast Region

Miami

Miami is located in southeastern Florida on the Atlantic coast. It is sandwiched between the Florida Everglades and Biscayne Bay. Downtown Miami is the heart of the city.

Miami's surrounding areas are partitioned into various sections. They include Brickell, The Roads, Little Havana, Watson Island, Coral Way, Virginia Key, Port Miami and several others. Each part of Miami is often a concentration of one or two particular industries.

Downtown hosts many national and international banks, financial companies' headquarters and civil courthouses. In fact, downtown has the largest number of international banks in such a tight concentration, in the US.

Miami is a leader in commerce, finance, media, entertainment, international trade and the arts. For both professionals and general workers, Miami typically advertises a wide variety of career and job opportunities.

Miami's cost-of-living is 118.70 compared to a US average of 100. This means that it's much more expensive to live in Miami than the average US city. The average listing price for a home in Miami is $471,000. The median sales price, as of mid-2014, was $215,000. Of its most popular neighborhoods, Southwest Coconut Grove had the highest listing price, with an average of $1.8 million. The lowest real estate price average was in Coral Way at $591,000.

Miami is truly an international resort city. Visitors constantly flock here from all over the world, which makes it an exceptionally diverse ethnic city. But the influence of its large Hispanic population is clearly woven into the fabric of Miami life and culture.

It is a destination for international arts, sports and entertainment. It is home to its own professional football, basketball and baseball teams, not to mention nationally ranked collegiate sports teams of every sort. Some of the world's finest golf, tennis and other sporting facilities can be found here. And boating enthusiasts of very type, including power boaters, sailors, kayakers and paddle boarders regularly come here to both have fun in the water and attend trade shows/expos.

South Beach is the epitome of what many imagine when they conceive of a wild beach playground for adults. It's a major tourist magnet, all by itself, as there is something interesting, unique and original or just plain entertaining to see practically all the time.

Southeast Region

South Beach is essentially a major entertainment destination. The beach and nearby streets are lined with restaurants, boutiques, hotels and nightclubs. Singles and young couples especially enjoy spending days on the beach and then enjoying the nightlife afterwards.

The area has an endless number of events and unique locations. These include fashion shows, scientific displays, concerts and the Overtown Rhythm - Arts Festival. Additionally, there are local artisan sites, venues for kids to do hand-on activities and places to watch new or classic movies.

Miami is certainly one of the most vibrant, busy, active, robust, touristy and pricey places to live. . The culture, concerts, dining, live entertainment and party atmosphere are non-stop. There are few places like it anywhere on earth, especially when one takes into account that it's in tropical Southeast Florida. For those drawn to this unique lifestyle, Miami is a great place to live.

Pembroke Pines

Pembroke Pines is the second most populated city in the greater Miami area. It is just a short driving distance away from lovely beaches, large lakes and neighboring rivers. The Everglades are to its west and there is easy access to Interstate 75 to its east. In addition to being only minutes away from the beach it is also a short drive from Miami and Fort Lauderdale.

Its warm weather makes for year-round summers, with temperatures in the 80s and 90s. If cool weather ever makes it to Pembroke Pines it usually only dips temperatures into the 70s.

Neighborhood streets here are often lined with tall draping royal palms. And there are still signs the area was once predominantly agricultural and rural. The layout of the sections in this city is part of what gives it the feel of a small town while actually being home to over 150,000 residents. National magazines have even awarded Pembroke Pines with titles such as, "100 Best Places to Live," and "#1 in Florida as Best Place to Raise Your Kids."

There are nearly 30 pristine parks in Pembroke Pines that feature beautiful landscape, walking trails and bike paths. This makes for lots of easily accessible places for outdoor fun, including watersports. Golfing however, is also extremely popular in local communities here.

The average cost of living in Pembroke Pines is 110.10 compared to the national average of 100. This means that it's significantly more expensive to live here than the average US city. Anyone purchasing real estate in Pembroke can expect to spend between $200,000 and $300,000. The average listing price, as of mid-2014, was $283,000 and the median sales price was $200,000. The two least expensive zip codes were 33312, with an average listing price of $390,000, and 33027, with an average listing price of $319,000.

Because of its location Pembroke Pines' job opportunities also include those in the greater Miami area. At any given time there are often thousands of posted job openings for qualified candidates. These include opportunities in insurance, management, healthcare, customer service and sales along with many hospitality positions catering to the many people that visit the greater Miami area each year.

For retirees who do not want to invest in pricey real estate there are several retirement communities in Pembroke. Gateway Terrace is located on 6th Avenue in Fort Lauderdale, Imperial Club is located on 183rd Street in

Southeast Region

Aventura and St. Andrews Place is located just outside of town in Miramar. All of these are just a short distance away from the heart of Pembroke Pines.

Pembroke Pines bills itself as somewhere residents live in order to enjoy a small town feel with access to big city amenities. For those who want to live in the Miami area, but do not want to live within the big city Pembroke is a much more laid-back alternative. It allows you the opportunity to raise your family in a more family oriented area with plenty of opportunities to work locally.

Many retirees especially like the option of having top-rated retirement communities in the city. This is a quieter place to live with quick access to the greater Miami area and all that is available.

Plantation

Many residents in the city of plantation claim it has an environment that is unsurpassed by any other south Florida city. Among its beautiful trees and lush landscapes are family-friendly neighborhoods, well-kept parks and a seemingly never-ending array of things to do. The city's official motto is "The Grass is Greener".

The city is noted for having some of the most beautiful parks in Florida, although trees can be seen everywhere ones looks. Some of its most popular parks enjoyed by locals include Volunteer Park Community Center on Sunrise Boulevard, Plantation Heritage Park on Fig Tree Lane and Liberty Tree Park on 16th Ave. Plantation Heritage Park is especially lovely, featuring rows of rare fruit trees and over 88 acres of various tropical plant varieties.

Each month, the city and local businesses partner in sponsorship of community events. Kids enjoy offerings that include spring break camps, tennis camps, equestrian camps and there is a Bring Teddy Bear picnic at the Plantation Library for very young children.

Family oriented events that take place each year include: the Daddy-Daughter Sock Hop and the Mother-Son Hoedown (both of which are held downtown), art shows at the park and special gatherings at local museums. Both civic leaders and emphasize the importance of family throughout Plantation communities on a regular basis. Families spending time together out in public are a regular part of the landscape in Plantation.

The average cost of living in Plantation is rated 97.40 compared to the US average of 100. This means it's considered slightly less expensive to live here than the typical US city. The average real estate listing price as of mid-2014 was $374,000. The median sales price was $241,000. And the most affordable zip code in the area was 33027, with an average listing price of $319,000. The most expensive area to live in was the 33304 zip code, with an average listing price of $750,000.

Because of its close proximity to Miami area job opportunities also include those within the big city. Many Plantation residents also work in nearby Fort Lauderdale as well. Sales, management, healthcare, customer service and information technology jobs are always advertised for those who qualify. Two of the largest employers in the area are HCA-East Florida (the largest healthcare provider Florida) and Robert Half Technology.

Plantation, Florida is truly a family-friendly city. Residents have purposed that it be a place where parents and children can have fun together, along with neighbors and close friends. Few cities can boast about sponsoring an annual mother-son day like Plantation does.

Locals are always pleased to have access to first class recreational facilities in addition to premier outdoor spaces.   Golfing, swimming and sports are also ever-popular things to do in Plantation.

Plantation is home to families, singles and retirees alike.   But its atmosphere is very much geared towards cultivation of family life. Residents enjoy its somewhat lower cost of living and scenic parks on a daily basis. This city offers a true sense of community amid the some of the prettiest surroundings found anywhere.

West Palm Beach

Because of swamplands just to its west, West Palm Beach is only a few blocks wide. But that very narrow piece of land has grown into a truly lovely city. As one might expect, the area is covered with many beautiful, tall royal palms lining beaches, waterways and streets. Many residential properties also feature these signature trees, which are an ever-present fixture upon the landscape.

There is much to see and do in West Palm Beach. On one hand, it's simply a beautiful place. The city's coastal location lends itself to both pristine white beaches and turquoise colored waters.

There are two noticeably distinct seasons here in West Palm – a wet season that is hot and humid, with rain showers and thunderstorms each afternoon, and a dry season that is mostly warm, with temperatures in the 80s. West Palm Beach summers generally reach highs in the 90s and though the area experiences almost a year-round summer it does occasionally have a cold front that passes through, with temperatures dipping as low as the 40s.

The average cost of living in West Palm Beach was rated, in mid-2014, at 99.30 out of a national average of 100. This puts it at about the same cost of living as any average US city. The average real estate listing price was $351,000, but the median sales price was much lower at $141,000. The Century Village neighborhood offered the most affordable home averages in the area at $36,000. Slightly higher than that is Golden Lakes with an average listing price of $80,000.

At the time of this writing there were hundreds of job opportunities throughout West Palm Beach. Those included positions in healthcare, sales, management, customer service, nursing and hospitality. One of the area's largest employers is HCA-East Florida, which is Florida's largest healthcare provider.

The West Palm Beach public school districts are considered to be among the best in Florida. Palm Beach County is Florida's highest performing urban public school district with a higher percentage of "A" and "B" rated schools than any other county.

Nature lovers love visiting nearby places such as McCarthy's Wildlife Sanctuary on 61st Street and the Grassy Waters Nature Preserve and Mounts Botanical Gardens, both just a short drive from the West Palm Beach area. And most kids love visiting the Palm Beach Zoo.

For those looking for something less vigorous, there is always something to do. There are regular outdoor festivals throughout the area, in addition to lovely shopping districts complete with less formal eateries and elegant restaurants for fine dining.

Downtown West Palm Beach is considered to be its hottest spot though. It is home to both a retail district and an entertainment district. There are often free concerts in the entertainment section accompanied by all types of vendors and arts-crafts artisans. The nightlife here also features a myriad of clubs, martini bars, upscale boutiques and fine dining (by candlelight) establishments.

West Palm Beach has a luxurious feel to it even though it's less pricey to live here than many other beach resort cities. This is one reason why many residents have chosen to live here. More than a few beach lovers now call this place home.

Florida Keys

The Florida Keys are part of an ancient, now exposed, coral reef in the south of Florida. The keys have more of a truer tropical climate than anywhere else in the Continental US; they are the only place in Florida that never frosts.

The two main seasons in the Keys are the dry season and the wet season. The wet season takes place between June and October. It's hot, humid and has rainfall almost every afternoon. From November to May the weather is much dryer with cooler temperatures, often dropping into the 70s.

Each year, the keys are threatened with tropical storms and hurricanes alike. During larger storms many residents are evacuated to the mainland. Due to the low elevation of the key when a huge storm makes landfall it can cause extensive flooding. Because of this threat many homes are built on concrete stilts. These lifted homes have become a stylistic staple throughout the region.

Fishing in the keys is, by far, some of the best in Florida. It is one of the island chain's major industries. Tourism is also an economic staple here. Ecotourism is particularly popular because of the area's protected waters, where free-divers and scuba divers enjoy countless views of incredible wildlife.

The keys are home to America's only natural living coral barrier reef. The best diving locations are about 5 miles offshore. The waters are crystal clear and contain an abundance of fish and other marine life. Many of these creatures make old ship wrecks throughout the area their home.

Many people choose to live in the keys because of their easy accessibility to the mainland, yet their communities are seemingly far removed from the rest the world. The Overseas Highway connects all of the keys with roads and bridges; it even features one of the longest bridges in the world. While driving through the keys and crossing its bridges you can often see a distinct turquoise color on the Atlantic side of the bridge and an emerald-green color on the Gulf side of it.

Ponce de Leon charted the keys in the early 1500s. After he discovered them they became an outpost for trade with Native Americans living there, both in the Bahamas and Cuba. This keys trade route eventually became a main trade route for those living as far away as New Orleans. Businessman Henry Flagler completed a railway running throughout the keys in the early 1900s. This transportation system helped develop the islands into thriving communities.

An organization referred to as the Conch Republic claims to be a micro-nation within the Florida Keys. It's an idea cultivated more for tourist purposes than genuine political independence. Key West is its supposed capitol. The republic's motto is "We Seceded Where Others Failed".

Florida Keys

Many local residents in the keys aspire to live their version of "the good life" or "the island life" in this region. They can routinely watch beautiful sunsets, enjoy swimming and boating with dolphins always somewhere nearby, fish in some of the richest fishing spots in the world and snorkel or deep dive in a world-famous barrier reef.

Residents who aren't addicted to watersports or lots of activity also love living here because it's almost impossible to be bored here. Even if one simply lounges on the beach, locals often enjoy the comradery of friends doing exactly the same thing.

Other activities common in the keys include museum visits, nature walks, sightseeing and shopping. In fact, shopping is sort of a unique experience in the keys. One can always seem to find plenty of starfish, shells and shark's teeth in souvenir shops. The most popular shopping areas in Key West are Clinton Square and Conch Plaza. Brightly colored storefronts are most likely decorated to the hilt with tropical-themed odds and ends adorning buildings and walls everywhere. Inviting streets are always places to see interesting things or meet interesting people – many from around the world.

Florida Keys

If every-day life in the keys isn't exciting enough, there are a bunch of year-round events in the keys that many residents participate in and enjoy a great deal. Key West plays host to a "History of Tourism" on Front Street every September. There are also numerous fishing tournaments in this area, where anglers seek out 40+ species of fish from April through November. Depending on the size of the catch, participants in these tournaments may receive awards and certificates for their achievements. Airshows are also popular year-round events here in the keys. And gardens such as the "Key West Tropical Forest and Botanical Garden" host annual garden parties.

Most people move to the keys in order to pursue their version of a tropical lifestyle they've probably dreamed about. And who can blame them? In a place filled with beaches, breathtaking sunsets, boating, swimming, nature and wildlife that include an abundance of dolphins and sea turtles, it's hard for many to not want to live here. It's a special place that most of those living here would gladly choose to do again and again.

Florida Keys

Key Largo

Key Largo is located in the upper Florida Keys. It's closest to the mainland and connected to Miami and the larger area of Dade County. Those living in the key have named it the "Diving Capitol of the World" because of the coral reef lying 5 miles off its shore. This reef attracts thousands of sport-fishing and scuba diving eco-tourists every year and is one reason why many of its residents choose to live on this island instead of one of the others.

Like the other Florida Keys, Key Largo features lovely blue-green waters and pure white beaches. To give many homeowners direct access to open waters, Key Largo officials created neighborhoods with extensive canals. Many of residents have boats and other forms of personal watercraft docked in their own backyards.

Many scuba divers plunge into the waters around Key Largo in order to enjoy legions of colorful schools of fish along the reef. Divers also seek out a unique statue submerged under the water known as "Christ of the Abyss." It's a bronze statue of Jesus Christ submerged in 25 feet of water about 5 miles east of Key Largo's coast. This statue, along with numerous shipwrecks in the area, allow for some spectacular diving sights. Both residents and tourists from around the world are attracted by the scenic beauty and wildlife specifically found in this place.

The average cost of living in Key Largo is 145.70 compared to the national average of 100. This means that it is much more expensive to live here than the average US city. The average real estate listing price and median sales price on this island is completely different. The average listing price is $1.1 million and the median sales price is under $400,000. Of the most popular zip codes, the area including 33035 has an average listing price at just a little over $650,000.

There are several elementary schools throughout the keys. And Coral Shores is home to the top-rated high school in the area, although many high-schoolers attend Key West High. There are also a number of charter schools in the area that offer parents more options in the way of public schooling.

Aside from the occasional hurricane evacuation drill, Key Largo is certainly recognized as one of the best places to live in the Florida Keys. The big city of Miami is readily accessible but yet also seems very distant, which is something many residents really like.

Key Largo is home to beautiful beaches, winding creeks, palm trees, tropical hardwoods, a marine sanctuary, one national park and 2 state parks. It also offers some of the best botanical scenes and foliage that can be found in the entire State.

There is never a shortage of things to do here. Swimming, snorkeling, scuba diving, fishing, eco-touring, and dolphin encounter programs are all readily available for water-lovers. And land-lubbers never tire from the nature trails, wild birds and other moving scenery that comes with living here. It's hard to imagine a better place to go biking, sailing or beachcombing for those attracted to this sort of lifestyle.

Florida Keys

Marathon Key

Marathon Key is actually a city consisting of several different small islands. These include: Grassy Key, Knight's Key, Key Vaca, Boot Key, Fat Dear Key, Crawl Key and Long Point Key. The city consists of a total area of just 9.6 square miles.

The key's tropical climate features summer year-round, with highs in the 80s and 90s. (There has never been a recorded snow, frost, or freeze in this city). As the rest of the US experiences lots of cold during winter months, residents in Marathon Key are going through the "dry season." It lasts from November to April with hardly any rain. The wet season lasts between May and October with rainfall nearly every day.

Like the other Florida Keys, Marathon Key is home to some beautiful white beaches and stunning clear blue waters. But it's not really a "quaint little tropical island paradise." Marathon instead has the atmosphere of a busy town. There seems to always be something going on here.

Real estate in Marathon varies, with its most popular zip codes averaging listing prices between $600,000 and $1.1 million. The average listing price for the entire key is $539,000 and the median sales price is $320,000. The least expensive zip code in the area is 33050 with an average listing price of $655,000.

Florida Keys

The average cost of living on Marathon Key is 130.50 compared to the US average of 100. This average shows that it is significantly more expensive to live on this key than the average US city.

Parents moving to the area have three main schools to choose from: Stanley Switlik Elementary, Marathon Lutheran School on 122nd Street and Marathon High School on Sombrero Beach Road.

To give as many residents access to the water as possible, many properties here are able to access canals that were dredged to provide a path to the ocean. This, of course, resulted in unique looking neighborhoods. Just about every row of houses is near a canal where homeowners can dock a boat (if they have one).

Many locals and tourists specifically enjoy Marathon Key for its sport fishing. Local charters depart from Marathon and head into the waters of both the Atlantic and Gulf of Mexico every morning. But natural reefs surrounding Marathon make it a popular spot for all types of outdoor activities, including: swimming, snorkeling, spearfishing, diving, and bird watching.

It's a generally great area to view wildlife of all sorts. A well-known sea turtle hospital in

Florida Keys

Marathon (which you can visit) releases turtles back into the wild after they've been nursed back to health following injury. And several local businesses provide eco-tours throughout the area.

Marathon hosts several events every year, some of which are now a part of its cultural life. The Seafood Festival is held every March, followed by tarpon fishing tournaments in April and May. There are other fishing tournaments every June and September. The Dockside Americana Music Festival takes place every July. And lighted boat parades typically accompany Christmas and New Year's holidays here.

If you're looking for an active, exciting place to live, right in the middle of the Florida Keys then Marathon may be the spot for you. There is always something to see, do or enjoy. If you can afford the lifestyle here then you're encouraged to investigate this intriguing, fun-filled place more to see if it's right for you.

Florida Keys

Key West

Key West is the southernmost city in both Florida and the continental US. The city of Key West encompasses the small island that ends the chain of inhabited islands in the Florida Keys.

The average cost of living in Key West is 150.60 out of a US average of 100. This means that it is significantly more expensive to live in the area than the average US city. Real estate on Key West runs quite high with an average listing price of $841,000 and a median sales price of $400,000. Two of the most expensive zip codes are 33037 and 33036, both of which have an average listing price of $1.1 million.

Many homes in Key West are stunning to look at. Not only are they colorful, but they're true architectural treasures. Bright color schemes are what one would expect to see on a tropical island. Many homes are shades of yellows, teals and blues, and shaded by tall draping royal palms.

Old Town Key West is also known for its colonial homes that are reminiscent of New Orleans. Downtown streets and shopping centers also keep with the tropical vibe with brightly colored storefronts and awnings.

It's also quite common for homes here to be lifted on concrete stilts to prevent flooding during tropical storms or hurricanes. These lifted homes have become stylistic staples of the keys.

For those who are considering moving to the area who have children Key West has top-rated public schools. Key West Montessori Charter School is the highest-rated school in the area. And Sigsbee Charter School is the second highest rated school located in the city.

Because of the many tourists that come to the area, jobs in areas such as hospitality, customer service and sales jobs are quite common among residents. Other advertised jobs in Key West include ones in engineering, information technology and banking.

There are many self-employed persons and small business owners on the island who earn income performing work that support the tourist industry. Such tasks are often quite mundane, while others offer tourists some of the best experiences of their lives. Boat charter operators, for example, take thousands of visitors out to the reefs near Key West every year.

Full-time residents come from all over the United States. But Key West also draws lots of individuals who stay for a while before moving on, including artisans, writers and treasure divers to its shores. Imagine all of the stories that are told each day on this island from people with such a wide variety of experiences. Such diversity makes it a very interesting place to live. Casual conversations with strangers often turn into an unexpected cultural experience.

Popular activities in Key West include: boating, golfing, shopping, and all-around sightseeing. There are also a variety of natural habitats for wildlife and bird watchers.

But let's face it. Lots of residents love this place because they love a good party. If you live here then you're always going to be able to find a place to be entertained. There cafes, open bars and pubs, plus venues for comedy, drama and music.

Very few people will ever live in such a diverse beachside town. If you're attracted to a place that combines idyllic beaches, practical businesses, vibrant cultural life and endless festivity then Key West might be the place for you.

For further reading about Florida ...

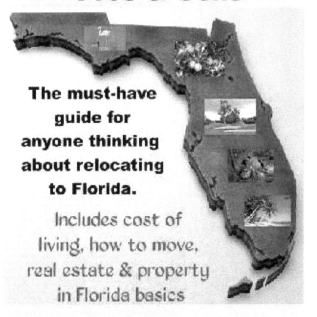

Moving to Florida
Pros & Cons

The must-have
guide for
anyone thinking
about relocating
to Florida.

Includes cost of
living, how to move,
real estate & property
in Florida basics

Dagny Wasil

CPSIA information can be obtained
at www.ICGtesting.com
Printed in the USA
BVHW040522010421
603820BV00010B/713